The Ultimate Guide to Rebuilding a Civilization:

Dynamic Practices and Core Principles for Building a Sustainable and Ethically Grounded Future

(Independent Living Series)

PUBLISHED BY Eagle's Nest Editions

© Copyright 2024 - All rights reserved.

Table of contents

Introduction

"In the end, we will remember not the words of our enemies, but the silence of our friends." – Martin Luther King Jr.

These words resonate deeply with the theme of this book. They remind us that, in times of crisis, it is not the malevolent forces we face that will shape our destiny, but the actions—or inactions—of those we rely on. As we embark on this journey together, consider this quote as a call to action, urging you to prepare not just for yourself, but for your community, your loved ones, and for future generations who will inherit the world we rebuild.

Overview

This book, "The Ultimate Guide to Rebuilding Civilization," is more than a survival manual. It is a comprehensive blueprint for those who wish to not only survive but thrive in the aftermath of a societal collapse. It is a guide for those who understand that being prepared is not just about hoarding supplies, but about acquiring the knowledge, skills, and mindset necessary to reconstruct a functioning, sustainable society from the ground up.

Civilization, as we know it, is a fragile construct. History has shown us that even the mightiest of empires can crumble under the weight of internal strife, economic turmoil, environmental disasters, or external threats. The possibility of such a collapse may seem distant or improbable to many, but it is a reality that we must be prepared to face. Whether due to natural disasters, pandemics, economic breakdowns, or even global conflicts, the pillars of modern society could, at any time, be shaken to their core.

This book is structured around four overarching themes: **Survival**, **Sustainability**, **Independence**, and **Social Reconstruction**. Each theme represents a critical component of what is necessary to not only survive in the short term but to build a resilient and thriving community in the long term.

- **Survival**: The immediate response to a crisis, focusing on securing the basic needs of life—water, food, shelter, and security.
- **Sustainability**: The practices and systems that ensure long-term survival and self-sufficiency, from sustainable agriculture to renewable energy sources.
- **Independence**: The skills and knowledge necessary to live without reliance on the complex systems of modern society.

- **Social Reconstruction**: The rebuilding of societal structures—governance, education, healthcare—that are essential for a functioning and just community.

Purpose and Scope

The purpose of this book is clear: to provide you with a comprehensive guide to rebuilding civilization from scratch. Whether you are a survivalist, a prepper, a community leader, or simply someone interested in sustainability, this book is designed to equip you with the knowledge and tools necessary to rebuild in the aftermath of a societal collapse.

Our goal is to cover every aspect of what it takes to not only survive but to rebuild. This book will guide you through the initial stages of survival—securing water, food, and shelter—before moving on to more complex issues such as establishing governance, rebuilding infrastructure, and creating sustainable systems for the future.

This guide is not just for those with experience in survival or homesteading. It is written for everyone, from beginners who are just starting to think about preparedness to experienced preppers who want to ensure they have considered every angle. It is for anyone who understands the importance of being prepared, not just for themselves, but for their community and future generations.

The Importance of Historical Lessons

History is replete with examples of civilizations that have risen and fallen, often due to a combination of external pressures and internal weaknesses. The collapse of the Roman Empire, the decline of the Mayan civilization, and the fall of ancient Mesopotamia all serve as stark reminders that no society, no matter how advanced, is immune to collapse.

However, history also teaches us valuable lessons about resilience and recovery. Many societies have managed to rebuild after catastrophic events, often emerging stronger and more unified. These historical examples offer us a roadmap for how to approach the task of rebuilding our own civilization should the need arise.

The lessons of the past inform our approach in this book. By understanding the causes of previous collapses—be they environmental, economic, or social—we can better prepare for and mitigate similar challenges in our time. More importantly, by studying how past societies rebuilt and recovered, we can gain insights into the principles and practices that will be essential in our own efforts to rebuild.

Framework of the Book

This book is divided into ten chapters, each focusing on a critical aspect of rebuilding civilization. The structure is designed to guide you step by step through the process, from immediate survival needs to long-term social reconstruction. Here's a brief overview of what you can expect:

1. **Surviving the Collapse**: Understanding the causes and signs of societal collapse and the psychological impact it has on individuals and communities. This chapter covers the essentials of immediate survival: securing water, food, shelter, and self-defense.
2. **Establishing a Sustainable Food Supply**: Techniques for growing food, hunting, foraging, and preserving food to ensure long-term sustenance.
3. **Building and Maintaining Shelter**: How to construct and maintain shelters using available resources, including advanced techniques for sustainable building.
4. **Water Management and Sanitation**: Methods for finding, purifying, and managing water, as well as ensuring proper sanitation to prevent disease.
5. **Reestablishing Communication and Transportation**: Strategies for setting up communication networks and rebuilding transportation systems in a post-collapse world.
6. **Power and Energy Solutions**: How to harness renewable energy sources like solar and wind, and how to store and conserve energy.
7. **Rebuilding Governance and Social Structures**: The principles of establishing leadership, creating laws, and rebuilding a resilient community culture.
8. **Health and Medicine in a New World**: Establishing a community health system, using traditional and herbal medicine, and ensuring preventive healthcare.
9. **Education and Knowledge Preservation**: The importance of establishing education systems and preserving knowledge for future generations.
10. **Reconnecting with Nature**: Strategies for restoring natural ecosystems, practicing sustainable agriculture, and preparing for environmental challenges.

Each chapter is packed with actionable steps and practical advice, ensuring that you are not only prepared to survive but to thrive and help rebuild a sustainable and resilient society.

The Journey Ahead

As you begin this journey, it's important to prepare yourself mentally and emotionally for the challenges ahead. Rebuilding civilization is not a task to be taken lightly. It requires not only physical preparedness but also mental fortitude and a strong sense of purpose.

This book will challenge you to think critically, to plan thoroughly, and to act decisively. It will encourage you to take responsibility for your own survival and for the survival of your community. It will push you to develop new skills, to think creatively, and to adapt to changing circumstances.

But most importantly, this book is about hope. It is about the belief that, no matter how dire the circumstances, we have the ability to rebuild and to create a better, more sustainable world. It is about the power of community, of working together towards a common goal, and of the resilience of the human spirit.

The road ahead may be difficult, but it is a journey worth taking. By the end of this book, you will have the knowledge, the skills, and the confidence to face whatever challenges may come your way. You will be ready to not only survive but to lead the way in rebuilding a thriving, sustainable civilization.

So, take a deep breath, gather your resolve, and let us begin this journey together. The future is in your hands.

Chapter 1: Surviving the Collapse

In the face of societal breakdown, survival is paramount. This chapter guides you through the essential steps to secure your basic needs, protect yourself and your loved ones, and begin the journey of rebuilding in a world transformed.

1.1 Understanding the Collapse

When we think of societal collapse, images of sudden, catastrophic events often come to mind—natural disasters, wars, or economic meltdowns that send shockwaves through communities and nations. However, the reality of societal collapse is usually more complex and multifaceted. Understanding the potential causes, recognizing the signs of an impending collapse, and preparing for the psychological impact on both individuals and communities are essential first steps in ensuring your survival and that of those around you.

Common Causes of Societal Collapse

Throughout history, civilizations have risen and fallen, often due to a combination of factors that, together, overwhelm the systems that hold societies together. These causes can be broadly categorized into environmental, economic, political, and social factors, though they often overlap and exacerbate one another.

Environmental Causes: Environmental degradation is one of the most common precursors to societal collapse. Overpopulation, deforestation, soil erosion, and water scarcity are just a few examples of how human activity can undermine the natural systems that support life. Climate change, with its potential to alter weather patterns, cause sea levels to rise, and increase the frequency of extreme weather events, is a particularly modern concern that threatens to destabilize global societies.

Historically, civilizations such as the Mayans and the Easter Islanders collapsed due in large part to environmental mismanagement. For the Mayans, deforestation and soil degradation led to agricultural decline, exacerbating famine and social unrest. The Easter Islanders, on the other hand, overexploited their natural resources, leading to deforestation, loss of wildlife, and ultimately, societal breakdown.

Economic Causes: Economic collapse can result from a variety of factors, including hyperinflation, financial crises, and the depletion of critical resources. When economies fail, they often take with them the stability and order that societies depend on. The collapse of the Roman Empire, for instance, was precipitated by a combination of economic mismanagement, inflation, and overreliance on slave labor, which destabilized the economy and contributed to the empire's eventual downfall.

In modern times, the Great Depression serves as a reminder of how economic collapse can lead to widespread suffering and social upheaval. While the world eventually recovered from the Depression, it left deep scars and led to significant changes in economic policy and governance, illustrating how closely tied economic stability is to societal resilience.

Political Causes: Political instability and corruption can also lead to the downfall of civilizations. When governments fail to maintain order, provide basic services, or address the needs of their people, societies can quickly descend into chaos. The fall of the Soviet Union is a prime example of how political corruption, combined with economic decline, can lead to the collapse of a superpower. As the Soviet government became increasingly unable to manage the economic and political challenges it faced, the state disintegrated, leading to widespread hardship and the reconfiguration of power structures across the region.

Social Causes: Social decay, marked by increased inequality, loss of social cohesion, and moral decline, can also contribute to the collapse of societies. When the social fabric begins to unravel, trust between individuals and institutions erodes, leading to conflict and the breakdown of communities. The French Revolution, for example, was fueled by social inequality and the disconnect between the ruling class and the common people, ultimately leading to a violent upheaval and the restructuring of French society.

Signs of Impending Collapse

Recognizing the signs of an impending collapse is crucial for preparing and responding effectively. These signs often manifest as a combination of the factors mentioned above, creating a perfect storm that can overwhelm even the most resilient societies.

One of the earliest signs of collapse is the breakdown of infrastructure and public services. When roads, bridges, and utilities are not maintained, and when public services such as healthcare, education, and law enforcement begin to deteriorate, it is often a signal that the underlying systems supporting society are weakening.

Another key indicator is the loss of trust in institutions. When governments, financial systems, and social institutions are seen as corrupt or ineffective, people lose confidence in their ability to manage crises, leading to increased social unrest and the potential for violence.

Economic instability, such as rising unemployment, inflation, and scarcity of essential goods, is another warning sign. As people struggle to meet their basic needs, crime rates can increase, and social order can break down, leading to a downward spiral of instability.

Environmental degradation, while often slower to manifest, can also serve as a sign of impending collapse. Persistent droughts, declining crop yields, and the depletion of natural resources are all red flags that a society may be heading towards a crisis.

The Psychological Impact of Collapse on Individuals and Communities

The psychological impact of a societal collapse cannot be overstated. The loss of stability, security, and normalcy can lead to widespread fear, anxiety, and trauma. Individuals may experience a range of emotional responses, from denial and anger to despair and hopelessness. Communities, too, can be torn apart as people struggle to survive, trust erodes, and social cohesion breaks down.

In the early stages of collapse, denial is a common response. Many people will cling to the belief that things will return to normal, even as the signs of collapse become increasingly apparent. This denial can prevent individuals and communities from taking the necessary steps to prepare, leaving them vulnerable when the crisis fully unfolds.

As the reality of the situation sets in, fear and anxiety can take hold. The uncertainty of what lies ahead, combined with the loss of control over one's circumstances, can lead to heightened stress levels and panic. This, in turn, can exacerbate the collapse, as people make irrational decisions driven by fear rather than reason.

In the long term, the trauma of living through a collapse can have lasting effects on mental health. Depression, post-traumatic stress disorder (PTSD), and other psychological conditions can become widespread, particularly if the collapse is prolonged or particularly violent. Communities may struggle to rebuild trust and cohesion, as the shared trauma of the collapse creates divisions and conflicts that are difficult to heal.

Understanding the potential psychological impact of a societal collapse is essential for preparing both yourself and your community. Building mental resilience, fostering strong social connections, and developing a clear plan of action can help mitigate these effects and increase your chances of surviving and thriving in the aftermath of a collapse.

1.2 Immediate Survival Needs

When the fabric of society begins to fray and collapse is imminent or already in progress, the most immediate concern becomes survival. In such a scenario, all the luxuries and conveniences of modern life fade into insignificance compared to the primal needs of water, food, and shelter. Securing these basic necessities is the first and most crucial step to ensure that you and your loved ones can withstand the initial shock of a collapsing civilization.

Securing Water Sources

Water is the most critical resource for survival, as the human body can only survive a few days without it. In a post-collapse world, the reliable infrastructure that delivers clean water to your tap may no longer be functioning. Therefore, the first and foremost task is to secure a consistent and safe source of water.

In the immediate aftermath of a collapse, there are several strategies to find and purify water. If you live near a natural water source, such as a river, lake, or spring, you have a potential lifeline. However, even natural water sources may be contaminated, especially in a post-collapse environment where pollution and waste management systems have broken down. Therefore, all water should be treated before consumption.

Boiling water is one of the simplest and most effective methods of purification, killing most pathogens. If fuel is available, bring the water to a rolling boil for at least one minute. In higher altitudes, where water boils at a lower temperature, it is advisable to boil the water for three minutes.

In situations where boiling is not feasible, chemical treatment is a viable alternative. Water purification tablets, which typically contain iodine or chlorine, can be an effective short-term solution. Always follow the instructions on the packaging, as incorrect usage can render the water unsafe or ineffective against pathogens. Additionally, portable water filters, such as those using activated carbon or ceramic filters, can remove many contaminants, though they may not eliminate all viruses. It is wise to have multiple purification methods on hand, as redundancy is key in ensuring a reliable supply of safe drinking water.

Rainwater harvesting is another practical approach, especially in regions with frequent rainfall. Simple systems can be set up to collect rainwater from roofs or other surfaces, directing it into storage containers. As with other water sources, rainwater should be treated before drinking, particularly if it has been collected from surfaces that might be contaminated with debris or pollutants.

In more extreme scenarios, where natural water sources are scarce, it may be necessary to resort to methods such as dew collection or solar stills. Dew collection involves using cloth or other absorbent materials to gather moisture from plants or surfaces in the early morning hours, while solar stills use the sun's heat to evaporate and condense water from damp soil or vegetation. Both methods can be labor-intensive and yield limited quantities of water, but they can be lifesaving in arid environments.

Finally, it's essential to plan for long-term water storage. Properly storing water in large, food-grade containers can provide a buffer against periods when fresh water may not be immediately available. Water should be stored in a cool, dark place, and containers should be checked regularly for signs of contamination. Adding a small amount of chlorine bleach (without additives) to stored water can help prevent the growth of bacteria and algae, extending the water's shelf life.

Securing a dependable water supply is not just about finding and purifying water in the immediate aftermath of a collapse; it also involves establishing systems and habits that will sustain you over the long term. As you gather water, always think ahead—conserve as much as possible, be vigilant about potential contamination, and continually seek out and test new sources. Water is life, and in a collapsed society, it may be the single most valuable resource you possess.

Finding or Constructing Shelter

Shelter is the second most crucial element of immediate survival. In the absence of functioning infrastructure and services, the need to protect yourself from the elements and provide a safe, secure place to rest becomes paramount. The type of shelter you require will depend on your environment, available resources, and the specific challenges you face in the wake of societal collapse.

If you are fortunate enough to remain in your own home, your first task will be to assess and reinforce its defenses against both natural and human threats. Begin by securing all entry points—doors, windows, and any other potential access points. Reinforce weak areas with materials such as plywood, metal bars, or even makeshift barricades. Remember, a well-defended home not only protects you from the elements but also deters potential looters or other threats.

In cases where staying at home is not an option—whether due to safety concerns, environmental hazards, or other factors—finding or constructing alternative shelter becomes a priority. The first rule of shelter building is location, location, location. Choose a site that offers natural protection, such as a hillside, dense forest, or cave. These locations provide not only shelter from the wind, rain, and sun but also camouflage and a degree of security from potential threats.

If natural shelters are unavailable, you may need to construct your own. In a wooded area, a simple lean-to can be built using branches and leaves. This type of shelter is quick to assemble and provides basic protection from wind and rain. A more substantial option is a debris hut, which can be insulated with leaves, grass, and other natural materials to retain body heat in colder climates.

In open areas where natural materials are scarce, you may need to get creative. Tarps, ponchos, or even plastic sheeting can be used to create temporary shelters. If you have access to a vehicle, it can serve as a makeshift shelter, though it's important to ensure proper ventilation to avoid carbon monoxide poisoning if you run the engine for warmth.

For those in urban environments, abandoned buildings can offer shelter, though they come with their own set of risks. Always thoroughly inspect a building before entering—structural integrity, the presence of other people, and potential hazards like gas leaks or contamination must all be considered. Once inside, secure the building as best you can and establish a safe area where you can sleep, store supplies, and plan your next steps.

Long-term shelter considerations should also be addressed as soon as possible. In a post-collapse world, your temporary shelter may need to become a more permanent home. If you are staying in one place, start thinking about ways to improve your shelter's durability and comfort. This might involve digging a root cellar for food storage, reinforcing walls, or expanding your living space to accommodate more people or supplies.

It's also important to consider the psychological aspects of shelter. In a world turned upside down, having a safe space to retreat to can provide much-needed stability and mental health benefits. Even the most basic shelter can become a sanctuary if it is well-organized, clean, and familiar. Take the time to personalize your space—small touches like organizing your gear, setting up a comfortable sleeping area, or even creating a small "living room" can make a significant difference in your overall well-being.

Finally, always have a backup plan. No shelter is completely invulnerable, and circumstances may force you to leave even the most secure location. Identify potential fallback shelters in your area, and if possible, prepare them in advance with basic supplies and equipment. Knowing that you have a secondary option can provide peace of mind and increase your chances of survival if your primary shelter is compromised.

Emergency Food Supplies and Nutrition

The third pillar of immediate survival is food. While the human body can survive for several weeks without food, a lack of proper nutrition will quickly lead to physical weakness, impaired cognitive function, and increased susceptibility to illness—none of which you can afford in a post-collapse environment.

In the initial days and weeks following a collapse, your focus should be on using up perishable foods first. Refrigerated and frozen items will spoil quickly without electricity, so these should be prioritized in your meal planning. Cook and consume these foods while they are still safe, and consider ways to preserve any excess. Drying, salting, or smoking meats, for example, can extend their shelf life without the need for refrigeration.

Once perishable foods are depleted, your attention will shift to non-perishable food supplies. Ideally, you will have stockpiled a variety of foods that are both calorie-dense and nutritionally balanced. Canned goods, dried beans, rice, pasta, and grains are all excellent choices, as they have long shelf lives and require minimal preparation. It's important to rotate these supplies regularly to ensure that they remain fresh and to avoid spoilage.

Water is also a critical component of food preparation, particularly if you are relying on dried goods. Ensure that you have sufficient water stored not just for drinking, but also for cooking. Simple recipes that require minimal ingredients and water will become staples in your diet, so familiarize yourself with basic cooking methods such as boiling, steaming, and baking using improvised ovens or open fires.

Nutrition is another crucial consideration. While it's easy to focus on calories in a survival situation, maintaining a balanced diet is essential for long-term health. Vitamins and minerals found in fresh fruits and vegetables, for example, will be hard to come by, so plan accordingly. Canned vegetables, dried fruits, and multivitamins can help bridge the nutritional gap, but they are no substitute for fresh produce.

This brings us to the importance of foraging, hunting, and gardening. Even if you have a well-stocked pantry, these skills will become increasingly important as time goes on. Foraging for wild edibles can supplement your diet and provide essential nutrients. Learn to identify local plants that are safe to eat, as well as those that are toxic. Many common weeds and plants, such as dandelions, clover, and wild berries, are not only edible but also nutritious.

Hunting and fishing are other valuable skills, providing access to protein sources that may be scarce in a post-collapse world. If you are not already familiar with basic hunting techniques, now is the time to learn. Small game, such as rabbits, squirrels, and birds, can be hunted with minimal equipment, while fishing requires only a rod, line, and bait. Be sure to check local regulations and restrictions, even in a collapse scenario, as overhunting or overfishing can lead to depletion of these resources.

Gardening is perhaps the most sustainable way to ensure a long-term food supply. Even a small garden can produce a significant amount of food, provided you choose the right crops and manage your resources effectively. Focus on growing high-yield, easy-to-grow vegetables such as potatoes, carrots, beans, and leafy greens. If possible, start composting to create rich, fertile soil, and consider companion planting to maximize your garden's productivity.

In the absence of a garden, sprouting seeds and legumes indoors can provide a fresh, nutrient-rich food source with minimal space and resources. Sprouts are easy to grow and can be ready to eat in just a few days, making them an excellent addition to your survival diet.

In conclusion, securing immediate survival needs—water, shelter, and food—requires not only preparation but also adaptability. The strategies you employ will depend on your environment, available resources, and the specific challenges you face in a post-collapse world. By prioritizing these needs and developing the skills to meet them, you increase your chances of surviving the initial stages of collapse and laying the foundation for a more sustainable future.

1.3 Self-Defense and Security

As the initial shock of societal collapse begins to settle, the realization of a new and dangerous reality emerges—one where the security of you and your loved ones becomes paramount. In the absence of organized law enforcement and social order, self-defense and security are no longer theoretical concepts but essential components of daily survival. This section will delve into the strategies, tactics, and mindset necessary to protect yourself, your family, and your resources from a wide range of potential threats.

Basic Self-Defense Strategies

Self-defense begins with the awareness that you are your first and most reliable line of defense. The collapse of societal structures often leads to a vacuum of power, where the rule of law is replaced by the rule of force. In such an environment, understanding basic self-defense techniques and principles is crucial.

The first step in self-defense is developing a mindset of vigilance. This means being constantly aware of your surroundings, recognizing potential threats, and understanding the baseline behavior of those around you. In a post-collapse world, situational awareness becomes your greatest asset. By staying alert and attentive, you can often avoid dangerous situations before they escalate.

Physical self-defense training is also invaluable. While not everyone has the time or resources to become a martial arts expert, learning basic techniques can make a significant difference in a life-or-death situation. Focus on simple, effective moves that target vulnerable areas of an attacker, such as the eyes, throat, and groin. Remember, the goal of self-defense is not to engage in a prolonged fight but to disable your attacker long enough to escape or neutralize the threat.

In addition to physical techniques, the use of weapons may become necessary. Firearms are the most effective means of self-defense in many situations, but they require proper training and maintenance. If you own a firearm, ensure you are proficient in its use, understand its limitations, and practice regularly under various conditions. Firearms should always be stored safely but within easy reach, as seconds can make the difference between life and death in a critical situation.

For those who do not have access to firearms, improvised weapons can provide a means of defense. Knives, clubs, and even everyday objects like hammers or heavy flashlights can be used effectively in self-defense. The key is to be mentally prepared to use these tools if necessary and to practice how you might deploy them in an emergency.

Securing Your Perimeter

Securing your home or shelter against potential intruders is a critical aspect of post-collapse survival. In a world where traditional security systems may no longer function, you will need to rely on physical barriers, vigilance, and community cooperation to protect your perimeter.

Begin by conducting a thorough assessment of your home or shelter's vulnerabilities. Identify all entry points, including doors, windows, and other potential access routes, such as basements or attics. Reinforce these entry points with materials at hand—boards, metal bars, or even furniture can be used to block doors and windows. Installing makeshift alarms, such as cans on a string or bells on doors, can provide an early warning of attempted entry.

In addition to physical barriers, creating a layered defense around your perimeter is advisable. This can include fencing, barricades, and obstacles that make it difficult for potential intruders to approach unnoticed. If possible, establish a clear line of sight from your home to these perimeter defenses, allowing you to monitor activity and respond quickly if needed.

One of the most effective deterrents to intrusion is the appearance of occupancy and readiness. A home that looks occupied and well-defended is less likely to be targeted than one that appears abandoned or vulnerable. Consider keeping lights on at night (using solar-powered or battery-operated lights if necessary), and maintain a visible presence during the day. If you have neighbors, coordinating patrols or watch shifts can further enhance the security of your area.

Dealing with Potential Threats (Both Human and Environmental)

The threats you face in a post-collapse world are varied and often unpredictable. Human threats, including looters, desperate individuals, and organized groups, represent a significant danger, but environmental threats such as wild animals, fires, and natural disasters can be equally perilous.

When dealing with human threats, the first line of defense is often deterrence. A well-defended home, visible security measures, and a reputation for readiness can discourage many would-be intruders. However, deterrence alone is not always enough, and you must be prepared to take decisive action if your security is compromised.

If you find yourself facing an intruder, the principles of self-defense come into play. Your response should be swift, decisive, and proportionate to the threat. Remember, the goal is to protect yourself and your loved ones—not to engage in unnecessary violence. If the situation allows, issuing a clear warning before using force can sometimes de-escalate the encounter, but you must be ready to act if the warning is ignored.

In the case of organized groups or gangs, the situation becomes more complex. These groups often operate with a level of coordination and intent that makes them particularly dangerous. If you are aware of such groups operating in your area, consider forming alliances with neighbors or other community members. A well-coordinated community defense can be far more effective than isolated individuals acting alone.

Environmental threats also require careful consideration and preparation. Wild animals may become more aggressive or desperate in the absence of human activity, particularly in areas where food is scarce. Understanding the wildlife in your area, including their behaviors and habitats, can help you avoid dangerous encounters. Secure your food supplies to prevent attracting animals, and be aware of potential nesting or denning areas near your shelter.

Fire is another significant risk in a post-collapse environment. With fewer resources available to combat fires, even a small blaze can quickly become catastrophic. Ensure that you have fire extinguishers on hand and know how to use them. Clear flammable materials away from your home, and consider creating a firebreak if you live in an area prone to wildfires.

Natural disasters such as storms, floods, and earthquakes may also become more dangerous in a world without organized emergency services. Stay informed about the risks specific to your area and take steps to mitigate them. This might include reinforcing your shelter, creating an emergency evacuation plan, or stockpiling supplies in a safe location.

In conclusion, self-defense and security are critical components of survival in a post-collapse world. By understanding the threats you face and taking proactive steps to protect yourself and your community, you can significantly increase your chances of surviving not just the initial stages of collapse but the uncertain times that follow. Preparedness, vigilance, and the willingness to act are your best defenses in a world where the rule of law may no longer apply.

1.4 First Aid and Medical Preparedness

In the immediate aftermath of a societal collapse, access to professional medical care is likely to be severely limited, if not entirely nonexistent. Hospitals may be overwhelmed or shut down, and essential medical supplies could quickly become scarce. Under such conditions, the ability to administer first aid and provide basic medical care becomes a matter of life and death. This section will guide you through the essentials of first aid skills, creating a basic medical kit, and handling common injuries and illnesses that you are likely to encounter in a post-collapse environment.

Essential First Aid Skills

The first and most critical step in medical preparedness is acquiring the knowledge and skills necessary to administer first aid. In a world where professional healthcare may not be available, these skills could be the difference between life and death, not just for yourself but for those around you.

Begin by familiarizing yourself with the basics of first aid. This includes learning how to assess a situation and provide immediate care for common injuries such as cuts, burns, fractures, and sprains. Understanding how to control bleeding is particularly important, as severe blood loss can lead to shock and death if not promptly managed. Techniques such as applying pressure to a wound, using a tourniquet, and bandaging effectively are all essential skills.

Cardiopulmonary resuscitation (CPR) is another critical skill. In the event of a heart attack, drowning, or other incidents that result in the cessation of breathing or heartbeat, knowing how to perform CPR can save lives. Practice this technique regularly, as proper timing and technique are crucial for its effectiveness.

In addition to CPR, learn how to manage choking emergencies using the Heimlich maneuver, as well as how to treat shock, which can occur in response to severe injury, blood loss, or extreme stress. Shock is a life-threatening condition that requires immediate attention; knowing the signs—such as rapid pulse, pale or clammy skin, and confusion—and how to stabilize a person in shock can prevent the situation from worsening.

Another vital aspect of first aid is the ability to treat burns, which can be a common injury in a world where makeshift cooking and heating methods are in use. Understanding the different types of burns—first, second, and third-degree—and how to treat each type is essential. For instance, cooling a burn with running water (not ice) is effective for minor burns, while more severe burns require careful handling, sterile dressings, and potentially more advanced care.

For those in colder climates, knowledge of how to treat hypothermia and frostbite is crucial. Hypothermia occurs when the body loses heat faster than it can produce it, leading to dangerously low body temperature. Symptoms include shivering, confusion, and loss of coordination. Rewarming the person gradually, using warm blankets and dry clothing, is key to treatment. Frostbite, which occurs when skin and underlying tissues freeze, requires careful warming and protection of the affected areas.

Beyond these basics, it's important to understand the principles of infection control. In a post-collapse world, where sanitation and hygiene may be compromised, infections can spread rapidly. Learn how to clean and dress wounds properly to prevent infection, and recognize the signs of an infection—redness, swelling, pus, and fever—so that you can take action before it becomes severe.

Creating a Basic Medical Kit

Having the right tools on hand is just as important as having the knowledge to use them. A well-stocked medical kit is an indispensable resource that can greatly increase your ability to handle medical emergencies. When building your kit, focus on versatility and the ability to treat a wide range of injuries and conditions with the resources you have available.

Your medical kit should include a variety of bandages and dressings, such as adhesive bandages, gauze pads, and rolls, as well as larger trauma dressings for more severe injuries. Sterile gloves are essential to protect both the patient and the caregiver from infection during treatment. Include a supply of antiseptics, such as alcohol wipes, iodine, or hydrogen peroxide, to clean wounds and prevent infection.

In addition to these basics, your kit should contain medical instruments such as tweezers, scissors, and a digital thermometer. Tweezers are useful for removing foreign objects from wounds, while scissors can be used to cut dressings or clothing. A thermometer is critical for monitoring body temperature and identifying fever, which can be a sign of infection or other serious conditions.

Pain relief is another important consideration. Stock your kit with over-the-counter pain relievers such as acetaminophen, ibuprofen, and aspirin. These medications not only help manage pain but also reduce inflammation and fever. Include antihistamines for allergic reactions, as well as a supply of antidiarrheal medications and laxatives, as digestive issues can become common in stressful and unsanitary conditions.

If you have the means, consider adding more advanced supplies to your kit, such as a tourniquet, a CPR mask, and a suture kit for closing wounds. A splinting material, such as SAM splints or even improvised materials like sticks and cloth, can be invaluable for stabilizing fractures. For those with specific medical needs, such as diabetes or asthma, ensure that your kit includes an adequate supply of necessary medications and equipment, like insulin or an inhaler.

Don't forget about preventive care—include supplies for maintaining hygiene, such as hand sanitizer, soap, and water purification tablets. Oral rehydration salts are also useful for treating dehydration, which can occur as a result of illness or extreme conditions.

Finally, consider including a basic first aid manual in your kit. Even if you're well-trained, having a reference guide on hand can be invaluable in a high-stress situation. Manuals that include information on common post-collapse conditions, such as heatstroke, hypothermia, and dehydration, as well as more advanced procedures like wound care and infection management, are especially useful.

Handling Common Injuries and Illnesses Post-Collapse

In the aftermath of a collapse, the likelihood of encountering injuries and illnesses increases significantly. The absence of regular medical care, coupled with the harsh conditions of a post-collapse environment, means that even minor injuries or illnesses can quickly escalate into serious, life-threatening conditions. Knowing how to manage these issues effectively is critical for survival.

Cuts, scrapes, and lacerations are among the most common injuries you're likely to encounter. While these may seem minor, they can lead to serious infections if not properly treated. Begin by cleaning the wound thoroughly with clean water and antiseptic. Remove any debris, such as dirt or gravel, with sterile tweezers. Once the wound is clean, apply an antibiotic ointment if available and cover it with a sterile dressing. Change the dressing regularly and monitor the wound for signs of infection.

Burns are another common injury, particularly in environments where open flames or improvised heating and cooking methods are used. As mentioned earlier, the treatment of burns depends on the severity. For minor burns, cool the area with running water and apply a sterile dressing. For more severe burns, avoid breaking any blisters and seek advanced care as soon as possible. Keeping the burn area clean and protected from infection is vital.

Fractures and sprains can also occur frequently, especially in the rough and unpredictable terrain of a post-collapse world. If you suspect a fracture, immobilize the affected limb with a splint and avoid moving the person until professional help is available. For sprains, the RICE method—Rest, Ice, Compression, and Elevation—can help reduce pain and swelling. Always be cautious when handling potential fractures, as improper movement can exacerbate the injury.

Infections, including respiratory infections, gastrointestinal infections, and skin infections, are likely to become more prevalent in a post-collapse environment where sanitation is compromised. Respiratory infections, such as pneumonia, can be particularly deadly if untreated. Encourage rest, hydration, and the use of fever reducers, and seek out any available antibiotics if the infection becomes severe. Gastrointestinal infections, often caused by contaminated food or water, require immediate attention to prevent dehydration. Ensure access to clean water and use oral rehydration salts to treat dehydration.

Another common concern in a collapsed society is the spread of infectious diseases. Without the infrastructure for vaccination and public health monitoring, diseases that were once under control may resurface. Learning to recognize the symptoms of diseases such as cholera, typhoid, and tuberculosis is crucial, as is understanding how to isolate and treat affected individuals to prevent the spread of infection.

Chronic conditions, such as diabetes, asthma, and hypertension, also present significant challenges in a post-collapse world. If you or someone in your group has a chronic condition, it's important to stockpile necessary medications and understand how to manage the condition with limited resources. For example, individuals with diabetes may need to monitor their blood sugar levels more carefully, especially if their diet changes drastically, and those with asthma should ensure they have a supply of inhalers and know how to avoid triggers in their environment.

In the absence of professional healthcare, your ability to manage these common injuries and illnesses effectively will be a key determinant of your survival. By equipping yourself with the necessary skills, knowledge, and supplies, you can significantly improve your chances of navigating the medical challenges that are likely to arise in a post-collapse world.

1.5 Forming a Survival Group

In the chaotic and uncertain world following a societal collapse, the notion of "going it alone" is not only dangerous but often unsustainable. The complexities and challenges of survival in such an environment are best met through collective effort and cooperation. Forming a survival group—a community of individuals who pool their skills, resources, and strengths—can greatly enhance your chances of surviving and even thriving in the aftermath of collapse. This section will explore the importance of community in survival, how to identify and recruit members, and the roles and responsibilities within the group.

The Importance of Community in Survival

Human beings are inherently social creatures, and throughout history, communities have been the cornerstone of survival and progress. In the context of a societal collapse, the importance of community becomes even more pronounced. The sheer number of tasks required to ensure survival—securing resources, defending against threats, managing healthcare, and maintaining morale—can quickly overwhelm an individual or even a small family. A well-organized survival group can distribute these tasks, allowing for a more efficient and sustainable approach to survival.

One of the most significant advantages of forming a survival group is the diversity of skills and knowledge that members can bring to the table. In a group setting, individuals can specialize in different areas—one person may have medical expertise, another might be skilled in hunting and fishing, while another could excel in construction and repairs. This specialization allows the group to function more effectively, as each member contributes in a way that maximizes their strengths.

Moreover, a survival group provides a support network that is crucial for mental and emotional well-being. The psychological toll of surviving in a post-collapse world can be immense, with stress, fear, and grief taking a significant toll on an individual's mental health. Being part of a group offers emotional support, a sense of belonging, and shared responsibility, which can help mitigate the feelings of isolation and despair that are common in such situations.

Community also plays a critical role in defense. A well-organized group is far more capable of defending against threats—whether human or environmental—than an individual acting alone. Group members can take turns standing watch, devise coordinated defense strategies, and respond more effectively to emergencies. The presence of a group can also act as a deterrent to potential aggressors, who are less likely to target a well-defended community than an isolated individual.

Additionally, in a long-term survival scenario, a group is better equipped to undertake larger projects that would be impossible for an individual. This includes tasks such as building and maintaining infrastructure, growing food, and establishing trade with other groups. These activities not only enhance the group's chances of survival but also lay the groundwork for rebuilding a functioning society.

Identifying and Recruiting Members

The process of forming a survival group begins with identifying potential members. Ideally, you should start this process well before a collapse occurs, as building trust and establishing roles takes time. When selecting members for your group, consider both the practical skills they bring and their personal qualities. Look for individuals who are resourceful, adaptable, and capable of working well under stress. Character is just as important as skill—someone who is reliable, trustworthy, and cooperative will be far more valuable than a highly skilled individual who cannot work well with others.

Consider people within your existing social network—friends, family, neighbors, and colleagues—as potential group members. These individuals are often the best candidates because you already have a relationship with them, which can make it easier to establish trust and cooperation. However, be mindful of the dynamics within these relationships; not all friends or family members will be suited for the rigors of survival in a post-collapse world.

When approaching potential members, be clear about your intentions and the goals of the group. Discuss the benefits of forming a group and the responsibilities that come with it. It's important that everyone understands the commitment required and is willing to contribute. Honesty and transparency are key—everyone should be on the same page regarding the group's objectives, values, and expectations.

Skills are an essential consideration, but so is diversity. A well-rounded group should have a mix of abilities, including medical knowledge, tactical skills, practical trades (such as carpentry, plumbing, and mechanics), and agricultural experience. In addition to these practical skills, consider the importance of leadership and decision-making abilities. Every group needs individuals who can take charge in a crisis, make informed decisions, and mediate conflicts.

Once you have identified potential members, the next step is to hold discussions and possibly even group meetings to gauge how well everyone works together. This is an opportunity to assess interpersonal dynamics and resolve any potential issues before they arise in a survival scenario. It's also a time to start building trust—members should feel comfortable relying on each other and sharing responsibilities.

Roles and Responsibilities Within the Group

Once your group is formed, establishing clear roles and responsibilities is crucial for ensuring that everyone contributes effectively and that the group operates smoothly. While flexibility is important—members may need to adapt to changing circumstances—having defined roles can prevent confusion and ensure that all necessary tasks are covered.

Start by identifying the essential functions that the group needs to perform regularly. These might include security, food production, medical care, communication, and resource management. Assign roles based on each member's strengths and expertise. For example, someone with a background in medicine could take on the role of the group's primary medic, while someone with tactical training might be responsible for security.

In addition to primary roles, consider secondary roles or cross-training members in multiple areas. This ensures that the group remains functional even if a key member is incapacitated or unavailable. For instance, if the group's primary food producer falls ill, someone else should be able to step in and manage food-related tasks.

Leadership is another critical aspect of group dynamics. Decide early on how leadership will be structured. Will the group have a single leader, or will it operate under a council or committee system? How will decisions be made—by consensus, majority vote, or by a designated leader? Clarifying these structures and processes from the outset can prevent disputes and ensure that the group operates efficiently.

Regular communication is essential for maintaining group cohesion and addressing any issues that arise. Establish regular meetings or check-ins where members can discuss challenges, share updates, and plan for the future. This is also an opportunity to reinforce the group's goals and ensure that everyone remains aligned with the overall mission.

Finally, consider the importance of discipline and accountability within the group. In a survival situation, the stakes are high, and mistakes or negligence can have serious consequences. Establishing clear expectations and holding members accountable for their responsibilities is necessary for the group's overall well-being. However, this should be balanced with compassion and support—everyone will face challenges and difficulties, and a strong group is one that helps its members overcome these obstacles together.

In conclusion, forming a survival group is one of the most effective strategies for increasing your chances of surviving a societal collapse. By building a community that values cooperation, trust, and shared responsibility, you create a resilient and adaptable unit capable of facing the myriad challenges that a post-collapse world presents. Whether you are planning for short-term survival or long-term rebuilding, the strength and solidarity of your group will be your greatest asset.

Chapter 2: Establishing a Sustainable Food Supply

Sustaining life requires a reliable food source. This chapter explores how to establish a sustainable food supply through gardening, foraging, hunting, and preservation, ensuring your community thrives in the long term.

2.1 Gardening for Survival

In the wake of a societal collapse, the ability to produce your own food becomes not just a convenience but a necessity. Gardening for survival goes beyond the leisurely pursuit of horticulture; it is a critical skill that can mean the difference between life and death. Establishing a sustainable food supply through gardening requires careful planning, resourcefulness, and a deep understanding of your environment. This chapter will explore the essential principles of survival gardening, including selecting crops that thrive in various climates, maximizing yields with limited resources, and maintaining soil health through crop rotation and effective soil management.

Selecting Crops That Thrive in Various Climates

One of the first considerations in survival gardening is the selection of crops that are well-suited to your specific climate and growing conditions. Unlike modern agriculture, which often relies on intensive inputs and controlled environments, survival gardening must be adaptable to the natural conditions of your environment. This means choosing crops that are not only hardy and resilient but also capable of producing a reliable harvest under less-than-ideal circumstances.

Begin by assessing your local climate, including factors such as average temperature, rainfall, and growing season length. Different crops have varying requirements for temperature and moisture, so it's crucial to choose varieties that match your local conditions. For example, in cooler climates with short growing seasons, crops like potatoes, kale, and carrots, which are frost-tolerant and mature quickly, are ideal choices. Conversely, in warmer climates with longer growing seasons, crops such as sweet potatoes, okra, and tomatoes, which thrive in heat, may be more appropriate.

It's also important to consider the resilience of crops to common local challenges, such as pests, diseases, and extreme weather events. Heirloom and indigenous plant varieties, which have been naturally selected for local conditions over generations, are often more resilient than commercially bred hybrids. These traditional varieties are more likely to withstand the unique challenges of your environment and can be an invaluable resource in a survival garden.

Another key factor is the nutritional value of the crops you choose. In a survival scenario, your garden must provide not just calories but also essential vitamins and minerals to maintain health and energy. Leafy greens like spinach and chard are excellent sources of vitamins A and C, while legumes such as beans and peas provide both protein and essential amino acids. Root vegetables like carrots and beets offer important nutrients such as beta-carotene and folate, which are vital for immune function and overall health.

In addition to staple crops, consider planting a variety of herbs and medicinal plants. Herbs like basil, thyme, and oregano not only enhance the flavor of your meals but also have antimicrobial properties that can help prevent illness. Medicinal plants, such as echinacea, calendula, and garlic, can be used to treat common ailments when conventional medicine is not available.

Maximizing Yield with Limited Resources

In a post-collapse world, resources such as water, fertilizer, and space may be scarce. Therefore, maximizing the yield of your garden with minimal inputs is essential. Techniques such as companion planting, vertical gardening, and mulching can significantly increase productivity while conserving resources.

Companion planting is a traditional method that involves growing complementary plants together to improve growth, reduce pests, and enhance soil fertility. For example, planting beans alongside corn and squash (the traditional "Three Sisters" method) allows the beans to fix nitrogen in the soil, benefiting the corn and squash, while the squash provides ground cover that helps retain moisture and suppress weeds.

Vertical gardening is another effective strategy, especially in areas with limited space. Growing plants on trellises, arbors, or stacked planters allows you to make the most of available space and can increase yields per square foot. This method is particularly useful for crops like beans, peas, and cucumbers, which naturally climb and can produce abundant harvests in a small footprint.

Mulching is a simple yet powerful technique for conserving water, suppressing weeds, and improving soil health. By covering the soil with organic materials such as straw, leaves, or grass clippings, you can reduce evaporation, keep the soil temperature stable, and add valuable nutrients back into the soil as the mulch decomposes.

In addition to these techniques, it's important to practice water conservation in your garden. Collecting rainwater, using drip irrigation systems, and watering during the early morning or late evening can reduce water usage while ensuring that your plants receive the moisture they need to thrive.

Crop Rotation and Soil Management

Maintaining soil fertility is crucial for the long-term productivity of your garden. Soil that is overused or improperly managed will quickly become depleted of nutrients, leading to reduced yields and increased vulnerability to pests and diseases. Crop rotation and effective soil management practices are key to sustaining a healthy, productive garden over the long term.

Crop rotation involves changing the types of crops grown in a specific area of your garden from season to season. This practice helps prevent the buildup of pests and diseases that are specific to certain plants and reduces the depletion of particular nutrients from the soil. For example, after growing nitrogen-hungry crops like corn or cabbage, it's beneficial to plant legumes such as beans or peas in the same area the following season. These plants fix nitrogen in the soil, replenishing this essential nutrient and preparing the soil for the next cycle of crops.

In addition to crop rotation, consider incorporating cover crops, also known as green manures, into your gardening practice. Cover crops such as clover, rye, or vetch can be planted during the off-season to protect the soil from erosion, improve its structure, and add organic matter when they are turned under. These crops help maintain soil health by enhancing microbial activity, increasing nutrient availability, and improving moisture retention.

Composting is another critical component of soil management. By recycling kitchen scraps, garden waste, and other organic materials into compost, you can create a rich, nutrient-dense soil amendment that enhances fertility and structure. Composting not only reduces waste but also improves the quality of your soil, promoting healthier plant growth and higher yields.

Finally, it's essential to monitor the pH and nutrient levels of your soil regularly. Soil testing kits are relatively inexpensive and can provide valuable information about the health of your soil. Based on the results, you can adjust your soil management practices, such as adding lime to raise the pH or incorporating specific nutrients to address deficiencies.

By carefully selecting crops, maximizing yields with limited resources, and maintaining soil health through rotation and management practices, you can establish a sustainable and productive food supply in your garden. This foundation of food security will not only support your survival in the immediate aftermath of a collapse but also contribute to the long-term resilience and self-sufficiency of your community.

2.2 Foraging and Hunting

In a post-collapse world, where conventional food supplies may be disrupted or depleted, the ability to forage and hunt can be a critical means of securing sustenance. Foraging and hunting not only provide essential calories and nutrients but also reconnect us with the natural environment, teaching us to live in harmony with the land. This section will delve into the fundamentals of identifying edible wild plants, mastering basic hunting and trapping techniques, and effectively preserving and storing wild foods for long-term use.

Identifying Edible Wild Plants

Foraging is an ancient skill that has sustained human populations for millennia, long before the advent of agriculture. The ability to identify and harvest edible wild plants is invaluable in a survival scenario, offering a source of nutrition when cultivated crops are unavailable or insufficient. However, foraging requires a solid foundation of knowledge, as the natural world is replete with both edible and toxic plants, some of which can be difficult to distinguish.

The first step in foraging is to familiarize yourself with the local flora. Begin by studying a reliable field guide specific to your region, which can help you identify common edible plants, their habitats, and their seasonal availability. Many wild plants are highly nutritious, often containing higher concentrations of vitamins and minerals than their cultivated counterparts. For example, dandelion greens are rich in vitamins A, C, and K, while nettles are a good source of iron, calcium, and protein.

When foraging, it's crucial to apply the "Universal Edibility Test" to any plant you are unfamiliar with, especially in a survival situation. This test involves separating the plant into its parts—leaves, roots, stems, and flowers—and testing each part individually by touching it to your skin, lips, and tongue before consuming a small amount. This method can help you avoid consuming toxic plants, though it is not foolproof and should only be used as a last resort when no other food sources are available.

Some of the most reliable wild edibles include acorns, which can be leached of their tannins and ground into flour; cattails, whose roots and shoots are both edible; and berries like blackberries, raspberries, and elderberries, which are rich in antioxidants. Wild greens such as lamb's quarters, chickweed, and purslane are also highly nutritious and can be eaten raw or cooked. Additionally, mushrooms can be a valuable food source, but extreme caution is necessary, as many poisonous species closely resemble edible ones. Unless you have expert knowledge or access to a detailed guide, it's best to avoid wild mushrooms altogether.

Foraging also includes the collection of wild nuts, seeds, and tubers, which can provide essential fats and carbohydrates. Nuts such as walnuts, hazelnuts, and chestnuts are excellent sources of protein and healthy fats. Tubers like wild potatoes and Jerusalem artichokes are starchy and filling, making them valuable staples in a survival diet. These foods are often available in the fall, when other food sources may be dwindling.

It's important to forage responsibly to ensure the sustainability of wild food sources. Avoid over-harvesting any single plant, and always leave enough for the plant to reproduce and for other foragers and wildlife. Additionally, be mindful of the environment; trampling or damaging plants and ecosystems can have long-term consequences. By practicing sustainable foraging, you can help maintain the health of the environment and ensure that these resources remain available for the future.

Basic Hunting and Trapping Techniques

While foraging can provide a variety of plant-based foods, hunting and trapping offer access to protein-rich meat, which is vital for maintaining energy levels and muscle mass in a survival situation. Hunting and trapping require a different set of skills and knowledge, including an understanding of animal behavior, proficiency with weapons or traps, and the ability to process and preserve meat.

Before you begin hunting, it's essential to familiarize yourself with the types of game available in your area. Different animals have different habitats, behaviors, and peak seasons, all of which will influence your hunting strategy. For instance, deer are most active at dawn and dusk and are often found near water sources, while rabbits tend to feed at the edges of fields or in brushy areas. Understanding these patterns will increase your chances of a successful hunt.

The most common weapons used for hunting include firearms, bows, and slingshots. Firearms are the most effective at taking down large game like deer, elk, or wild boar, but they require ammunition, which may be scarce in a post-collapse world. Bows, particularly compound bows, are quieter and do not rely on ammunition in the same way, making them a useful alternative for both large and small game. Slingshots, while less powerful, can be effective for hunting small animals such as birds or squirrels and are easy to carry and conceal.

Trapping is another crucial technique, particularly for small game, and has the advantage of allowing you to hunt multiple animals simultaneously. Snares, deadfall traps, and pit traps are all effective methods for capturing animals. Snares, which are simple loops made from wire or cord, are especially versatile and can be set in various locations where animals are likely to pass through. Deadfall traps use a heavy object, such as a rock or log, that falls onto the animal when it triggers the trap, killing it instantly. Pit traps, on the other hand, involve digging a hole in the ground and covering it with branches and leaves to camouflage the opening; when an animal steps on the cover, it falls into the pit and becomes trapped.

When setting traps, it's important to consider the location carefully. Look for signs of animal activity, such as tracks, droppings, or disturbed vegetation, and set your traps in these areas. Check your traps regularly to avoid unnecessary suffering for the animals and to ensure that the meat is fresh when you retrieve it.

Processing game requires skill and knowledge to ensure that the meat is safe to eat and can be preserved for future use. After killing an animal, the first step is to field dress it, which involves removing the internal organs to prevent spoilage. This should be done as soon as possible after the kill. The meat can then be butchered into usable cuts, depending on the size and type of animal. For large game, this might involve separating the meat into quarters, while small game like rabbits can be skinned and gutted in one piece.

Preserving and Storing Wild Foods

Once you've harvested wild plants or game, preserving and storing these foods is crucial to ensure a stable food supply over time. Preservation techniques such as drying, smoking, salting, and pickling have been used for centuries and remain effective methods for extending the shelf life of food in the absence of refrigeration.

Drying is one of the simplest and most versatile methods of preservation, suitable for both plant-based foods and meat. For plant foods like fruits, vegetables, and herbs, drying can be accomplished by hanging them in a well-ventilated area out of direct sunlight, or by using a solar dehydrator. Meat can be dried to create jerky, a lightweight and portable food that can last for months when stored properly. Thinly slice the meat, season it with salt and spices, and then dry it over low heat or in the sun until it is completely dehydrated.

Smoking is another effective preservation method, particularly for meat and fish. The process involves exposing the food to smoke from burning wood, which not only dehydrates it but also imparts a smoky flavor and inhibits the growth of bacteria. Cold smoking, done at lower temperatures, is ideal for longer preservation, while hot smoking, at higher temperatures, cooks the food while also preserving it. Both methods require a smokehouse or smoker, which can be constructed from simple materials.

Salting is an ancient technique that relies on the antimicrobial properties of salt to preserve food. Salt draws moisture out of the food, creating an environment where bacteria cannot thrive. Meat can be salted by rubbing it with a generous amount of salt and storing it in a cool, dry place. The meat can then be soaked in water before cooking to remove some of the excess salt. Fish is often preserved by packing it in layers of salt and storing it in barrels or jars.

Pickling is another method that involves submerging food in a solution of vinegar, salt, and spices. The acidity of the vinegar creates a hostile environment for bacteria, allowing the food to be stored for extended periods. Vegetables such as cucumbers, peppers, and cabbage are commonly pickled, but fruits and even eggs can be preserved this way as well.

Root cellaring is a traditional method of storing root vegetables, such as potatoes, carrots, and onions, in a cool, dark, and humid environment. A root cellar can be as simple as a pit dug into the ground or a more elaborate underground room. The key is to maintain a consistent temperature and humidity level to prevent the food from spoiling. Root cellaring is particularly useful in regions with cold winters, where fresh produce would otherwise be difficult to obtain.

Finally, fermenting is a preservation technique that also enhances the nutritional value of food by promoting the growth of beneficial bacteria. Fermented foods such as sauerkraut, kimchi, and yogurt are not only preserved but also rich in probiotics, which support digestive health. Fermentation requires a controlled environment, usually at room temperature, and can take anywhere from a few days to several weeks, depending on the food and desired flavor.

By mastering these preservation techniques, you can create a stockpile of food that will sustain you through periods of scarcity, ensuring that you and your community have access to nutritious meals even in the most challenging conditions.

In conclusion, foraging and hunting are essential skills for establishing a sustainable food supply in a post-collapse world. By learning to identify and harvest wild plants, mastering basic hunting and trapping techniques, and preserving the food you gather, you can secure a reliable source of nutrition that complements your gardening efforts and enhances your overall resilience in the face of uncertainty.

2.3 Animal Husbandry

In a post-collapse scenario, animal husbandry can play a crucial role in ensuring a sustainable and reliable food supply. The ability to raise and manage livestock not only provides a consistent source of protein but also offers other valuable resources such as milk, eggs, wool, and manure, which can be used to enrich soil fertility. Establishing a system for raising animals requires careful consideration of the species best suited to your environment, the construction of appropriate shelters, and effective breeding and management practices. This section will guide you through the essential aspects of choosing the right livestock, building and maintaining shelters, and managing herds to ensure long-term sustainability.

Choosing the Right Livestock for Sustainability

Selecting the appropriate livestock for your circumstances is the first step in successful animal husbandry. The choice of animals will depend on various factors, including your geographic location, available resources, climate, and the specific needs of your survival group. It's important to choose animals that are hardy, easy to manage, and capable of thriving on available forage or minimal feed.

Chickens are one of the most versatile and low-maintenance livestock options for any survival situation. They require relatively little space, can forage for much of their food, and provide a steady supply of eggs, which are an excellent source of protein and essential nutrients. Additionally, chickens can be raised for meat, and their manure is highly beneficial for composting and enriching garden soil. Breeds such as Rhode Island Reds, Plymouth Rocks, and Leghorns are particularly hardy and productive, making them ideal choices for small-scale, sustainable farming.

Goats are another excellent option, particularly in areas where land is limited or where vegetation is sparse. Goats are highly adaptable and can thrive in environments where other livestock might struggle. They provide milk, which can be consumed directly or processed into cheese, yogurt, and butter. Goat meat is also a valuable protein source, and their manure, like that of chickens, is an excellent fertilizer. Goats are known for their ability to graze on a wide variety of plants, including brush and weeds, making them useful for managing overgrown areas. Breeds such as Nubian, Alpine, and Boer goats are well-suited for both milk and meat production.

Sheep are another versatile livestock option, particularly valued for their wool, which can be used for clothing, blankets, and other essential items in a survival situation. Sheep also provide milk and meat, making them a valuable addition to a sustainable farm. They are particularly well-suited to cooler climates and can graze on pasture, reducing the need for supplemental feed. Breeds such as the Dorset, Merino, and Suffolk are known for their productivity and hardiness.

Rabbits are an often-overlooked but highly efficient source of meat. They require minimal space, reproduce quickly, and can be fed a diet of forage, garden scraps, and hay. Rabbit manure is also an excellent fertilizer, rich in nutrients that can be directly applied to the garden without composting. Breeds such as New Zealand, Californian, and Flemish Giant are popular choices for meat production.

In addition to these common livestock choices, consider the potential of raising **ducks** or **geese**, which are less common but offer unique advantages. Ducks are excellent foragers, particularly in wet environments, and provide both eggs and meat. They are also less prone to certain diseases than chickens. Geese, on the other hand, are effective grazers and can act as natural weed controllers, while also providing meat and feathers.

When choosing livestock, it's important to consider not only the immediate benefits but also the long-term sustainability of the animals. Factors such as reproductive rate, feed efficiency, and the ability to withstand local diseases and pests are all critical. Additionally, consider the animals' potential contributions to the overall farm ecosystem—such as providing manure for compost or helping to manage pests through grazing or foraging.

Building and Maintaining Shelters for Animals

Once you have selected your livestock, the next step is to provide them with adequate shelter. Proper housing is essential for protecting animals from the elements, predators, and disease, as well as for ensuring their comfort and productivity. The design and construction of animal shelters will vary depending on the species, climate, and available materials, but some general principles apply across all types of livestock.

Shelters should provide protection from extreme weather conditions, including heat, cold, wind, and rain. In colder climates, shelters should be insulated or constructed with materials that help retain heat, such as straw or wood. In warmer climates, good ventilation is critical to prevent overheating and ensure a constant flow of fresh air. Consider building shelters with adjustable features, such as windows or vents, that can be opened or closed depending on the weather.

Chickens require a secure coop to protect them from predators such as foxes, raccoons, and hawks. The coop should include nesting boxes for egg-laying, roosting bars for sleeping, and enough space for the birds to move around comfortably. A general rule of thumb is to provide at least 2-3 square feet per chicken inside the coop, with additional space in an outdoor run. The coop should be raised off the ground to prevent moisture buildup and deter burrowing predators. Regular cleaning and maintenance are essential to prevent the buildup of ammonia from droppings, which can lead to respiratory issues.

Goats need a shelter that protects them from the elements while allowing them to roam freely. A three-sided shed is often sufficient in milder climates, while a fully enclosed barn or shed may be necessary in colder or wetter regions. Goats are notorious for their curiosity and climbing abilities, so shelters should be sturdy and secure to prevent escapes. Additionally, goats require space to graze and forage, so ensure that their shelter opens onto a secure pasture or paddock.

Sheep require similar shelter to goats, with the addition of shearing facilities if you plan to harvest wool. Their shelter should provide protection from wind and rain, and bedding such as straw should be provided to keep them warm and dry. Sheep are susceptible to foot rot, especially in wet conditions, so it's important to keep their shelter and surrounding area well-drained and clean.

Rabbits can be housed in hutches or cages, which should be elevated off the ground to protect them from predators and dampness. Hutches should include a sheltered area for sleeping and an open area with wire mesh for ventilation. If possible, provide rabbits with access to a secure outdoor pen where they can graze and exercise. Regularly clean and disinfect their living space to prevent the spread of disease.

In addition to shelter, all animals require access to clean water and a consistent supply of food. Water should be provided in containers that are easy to clean and prevent contamination from dirt or droppings. In colder climates, consider using heated water bowls or troughs to prevent freezing. Feed should be stored in a dry, secure location to protect it from pests and spoilage.

Maintaining animal shelters involves regular cleaning, repairs, and inspections to ensure the health and well-being of your livestock. Remove soiled bedding and waste regularly to prevent the buildup of harmful bacteria and parasites. Inspect shelters for signs of damage, such as holes or leaks, and repair them promptly to prevent predators from gaining access or to protect animals from the elements.

Properly designed and maintained shelters are crucial for the productivity and health of your livestock. They provide a safe and comfortable environment that supports their growth, reproduction, and overall well-being, ensuring a reliable source of food and other resources for your survival efforts.

2.4 Food Preservation Techniques

In a post-collapse world, ensuring a steady and reliable food supply is crucial, but equally important is the ability to preserve the food you harvest, forage, or hunt. Food preservation techniques, such as canning, pickling, dehydration, smoking, and root cellaring, are essential skills that allow you to extend the shelf life of your food, ensuring that you have access to nutritious meals even during periods when fresh food is scarce. This section will explore various food preservation methods, providing you with the knowledge and tools to store food effectively and safely for the long term.

Canning and Pickling

Canning is one of the most effective methods of preserving food, allowing you to store fruits, vegetables, meats, and even complete meals for years. The process involves placing food in jars and heating them to a temperature that destroys harmful microorganisms, creating a vacuum seal that prevents contamination. There are two main types of canning: water bath canning and pressure canning.

Water bath canning is suitable for high-acid foods, such as fruits, tomatoes, and pickles. The acidity of these foods helps prevent the growth of bacteria, making them safe to can using boiling water. To water bath can, you will need a large pot with a lid, a rack to keep the jars off the bottom of the pot, and canning jars with lids and bands. The process involves filling the jars with prepared food, leaving some headspace, sealing the lids, and then boiling the jars in water for a specified amount of time.

Pressure canning is necessary for low-acid foods, such as vegetables, meats, and soups. These foods require higher temperatures to safely preserve them, which can only be achieved with a pressure canner. A pressure canner is a specialized piece of equipment that uses steam under pressure to reach temperatures above boiling. The process is similar to water bath canning but involves sealing the jars in a pressure canner and processing them at a specific pressure and time. Pressure canning ensures that all bacteria, including the spores that cause botulism, are destroyed, making the food safe for long-term storage.

Pickling is another effective preservation method that relies on vinegar, salt, and spices to create an acidic environment that inhibits the growth of bacteria. Pickling can be done through **fermentation** or by using a vinegar brine. Fermentation pickling, such as making sauerkraut or kimchi, involves allowing the food to naturally ferment in a brine solution, producing lactic acid that preserves the food. This method not only preserves the food but also enhances its nutritional value by promoting the growth of beneficial probiotics. Vinegar pickling involves submerging food in a boiling vinegar solution and sealing it in jars. This method is quicker than fermentation and produces a tangy, flavorful product that can be stored for months.

Both canning and pickling require attention to detail and adherence to safety guidelines to ensure that the food is properly preserved and free from harmful bacteria. Always use clean, sterilized jars and follow tested recipes to ensure the correct balance of acidity, sugar, and salt. Improper canning or pickling can lead to foodborne illnesses, so it's important to familiarize yourself with the process and practice it regularly to build confidence and skill.

Dehydration and Smoking

Dehydration is a simple and effective way to preserve a wide variety of foods, including fruits, vegetables, meats, and herbs. By removing the moisture from food, you inhibit the growth of bacteria, yeast, and mold, which require water to thrive. Dehydrated foods are lightweight, easy to store, and retain most of their nutritional value, making them an ideal option for long-term food storage.

There are several methods of dehydration, including sun drying, oven drying, and using a food dehydrator. **Sun drying** is one of the oldest methods and is still effective in warm, dry climates. Foods like fruits, herbs, and thinly sliced vegetables can be spread out on screens or trays and left to dry in the sun. To protect the food from insects and dust, cover it with cheesecloth or netting. Sun drying requires several days of consistent warm temperatures and low humidity.

Oven drying is a more controlled method and can be done in any climate. To oven dry food, set your oven to a low temperature, typically around 140°F (60°C), and place the food on trays in a single layer. Leave the oven door slightly ajar to allow moisture to escape. The drying process can take several hours, depending on the food and thickness of the slices.

A **food dehydrator** is the most efficient method of dehydration, providing consistent heat and airflow to dry food quickly and evenly. Dehydrators come with adjustable temperature settings and multiple trays, allowing you to dry large quantities of food at once. Fruits like apples, bananas, and berries, as well as vegetables like tomatoes, peppers, and mushrooms, are all excellent candidates for dehydration. Once dried, store the food in airtight containers in a cool, dark place to maximize shelf life.

Smoking is another traditional method of preserving food, particularly meats and fish. Smoking involves exposing food to smoke from burning wood, which not only dehydrates the food but also imparts a smoky flavor and acts as a natural preservative. There are two main types of smoking: cold smoking and hot smoking.

Cold smoking is done at lower temperatures (below 90°F or 32°C) and is primarily used to flavor the food while still requiring additional preservation methods, such as curing or drying. Cold-smoked foods include items like smoked cheese, nuts, and cured meats like ham or bacon. Cold smoking typically takes several days and requires a smoker that can maintain low temperatures.

Hot smoking, on the other hand, cooks the food while smoking it, making it ready to eat immediately or store for later use. Hot smoking is done at temperatures between 150°F and 225°F (65°C to 107°C) and is ideal for meats like fish, poultry, and sausages. The smoking process can take several hours, depending on the type and thickness of the food. Once smoked, the food can be eaten immediately, refrigerated, or further preserved by drying or vacuum sealing.

Root Cellaring and Other Traditional Methods

Root cellaring is a time-tested method of storing vegetables and fruits in a cool, dark, and humid environment. Root cellars take advantage of the earth's natural insulation to maintain a stable temperature, usually between 32°F and 40°F (0°C to 4°C), and high humidity levels, which are ideal for storing root vegetables, apples, cabbages, and other produce that can last for several months.

To set up a root cellar, choose a location that is below ground or partially buried, such as a basement, shed, or even a pit dug into the ground. The key to a successful root cellar is maintaining the right conditions: cool, dark, and moist. Ventilation is important to prevent the buildup of ethylene gas, which can cause produce to spoil. Additionally, consider installing shelves or bins to keep the produce off the ground and allow air circulation around each item.

For those without access to a root cellar, **other traditional methods** of food preservation can be just as effective. **Fermentation** is a natural process that not only preserves food but also enhances its nutritional value. Foods like sauerkraut, kimchi, and yogurt are all products of fermentation, which involves the conversion of sugars into alcohol or acids by beneficial bacteria. Fermented foods are rich in probiotics, which support digestive health and can be stored for long periods without refrigeration.

Salting and curing are also traditional methods used to preserve meats, fish, and even vegetables. Salting involves packing food in salt, which draws out moisture and creates an environment that is inhospitable to bacteria. Curing is similar but often involves the addition of sugar, nitrates, or spices to enhance flavor and preservation. Both methods require careful control of temperature and humidity to prevent spoilage and ensure the food remains safe to eat.

Freezing is another effective preservation method, though it requires a reliable source of cold temperatures, such as a natural icehouse or a makeshift freezer in colder climates. Frozen foods can last for months or even years if properly stored, retaining much of their original flavor and nutritional value. However, in a post-collapse scenario, access to consistent freezing temperatures may be limited, so freezing should be used in conjunction with other preservation methods.

By mastering these food preservation techniques, you can build a reliable stockpile of food that will sustain you and your community through the most challenging times. Whether you are canning, dehydrating, smoking, or root cellaring, each method offers a way to extend the life of your food, reduce waste, and ensure that you have access to nutritious, home-grown meals even when fresh supplies are scarce.

Chapter 3: Building and Maintaining Shelter

Shelter is the foundation of security and well-being. In this chapter, you'll learn how to build and maintain safe, durable structures that protect against the elements and provide a sanctuary for your community.

3.1 Selecting a Location

In the aftermath of a societal collapse, securing a safe and reliable shelter becomes a top priority. Your shelter is not just a place to rest; it is your primary defense against the elements, a sanctuary from potential threats, and a cornerstone of your long-term survival strategy. The process of building and maintaining a shelter begins with selecting an appropriate location— one that offers not only physical protection but also access to essential resources like water, food, and materials for construction. This chapter will guide you through the strategic considerations for choosing a safe location, assessing natural resources and risks, and zoning your community for optimal functionality.

Strategic Considerations for Choosing a Safe Location

When selecting a location for your shelter, the first and most important consideration is safety. In a post-collapse environment, the risks you face can be numerous and unpredictable, including environmental hazards, human threats, and even wildlife. Your shelter's location should minimize these risks while maximizing your access to the resources needed for survival.

One of the primary considerations is **geographic elevation**. Choosing a location on higher ground offers several advantages. Elevated areas are less likely to flood, which is crucial if your region experiences heavy rainfall, snowmelt, or is near bodies of water. Additionally, higher ground can provide a strategic advantage in terms of visibility, allowing you to monitor your surroundings for potential threats and giving you more time to react. However, it's important to balance the benefits of elevation with accessibility—extremely high or difficult-to-reach areas may hinder your ability to gather resources or evacuate if necessary.

Another key factor is **proximity to water**. A reliable source of fresh water is essential for drinking, cooking, and sanitation. Ideally, your shelter should be within a short distance of a river, stream, or lake, but far enough away to avoid the dangers of flooding or waterborne diseases. If natural water sources are scarce, consider the feasibility of digging a well or setting up a rainwater harvesting system. Remember that water security is crucial for your long-term survival, so this should be one of the top priorities when selecting a location.

Access to food sources is also critical. If you plan to rely on foraging, hunting, or fishing, your shelter should be situated in an area with abundant wildlife, edible plants, and fishable waters. Forested areas often provide ample opportunities for hunting and gathering, while proximity to open fields or meadows can be beneficial for gardening and animal husbandry. Consider the sustainability of these resources as well—overexploitation can lead to scarcity, so choose a location where you can manage and renew these resources effectively.

Environmental hazards must be carefully assessed when choosing a location. Avoid areas that are prone to natural disasters such as earthquakes, landslides, or hurricanes. In regions where such events are common, look for areas with natural protection, such as hills or rock formations, that can shield you from wind, debris, or shifting earth. It's also wise to stay clear of industrial areas, which may become toxic in the event of a collapse, as well as regions with a history of environmental degradation.

The **climate** of the area should also influence your decision. Consider how the local weather patterns will affect your shelter and overall survival. In colder climates, you'll need to think about insulation and heating to survive harsh winters, while in warmer regions, ventilation and shade will be critical to avoid heatstroke and dehydration. If possible, select a location that offers some natural protection from extreme weather, such as a site with tree cover for shade or a south-facing slope for warmth.

Security is another paramount consideration. In a world where law and order may no longer exist, your shelter should be defensible against human threats. This means choosing a location that is not easily accessible or visible to outsiders. A remote location, or one that is naturally camouflaged by the landscape, can reduce the likelihood of being discovered by potential aggressors. Additionally, consider how you will secure the perimeter of your shelter—natural barriers like rivers or cliffs can provide added protection, but you may also need to construct fences or other fortifications to safeguard your home.

Finally, consider the **potential for expansion** and community development. While your immediate focus may be on creating a secure shelter for yourself and your family, it's important to think about the future. If conditions improve or you plan to establish a larger, self-sustaining community, you'll need space to expand your living area, grow food, and accommodate additional people. Choose a location that offers room for growth, whether that means building more structures, planting larger gardens, or raising more livestock.

In conclusion, selecting the right location for your shelter is a complex but crucial task that requires careful consideration of safety, resources, and long-term viability. By prioritizing these factors, you can establish a secure and sustainable base that will serve as the foundation for your survival and the potential rebuilding of your community. The right location not only provides immediate protection and resources but also sets the stage for resilience and growth in the face of an uncertain future.

3.2 Basic Construction Techniques

Once you have selected an ideal location for your shelter, the next critical step is the construction itself. The ability to build a sturdy, weather-resistant structure with limited resources is an essential skill in any survival scenario. Your shelter must provide protection from the elements, security against potential threats, and a level of comfort that supports physical and mental well-being. This section will guide you through basic construction techniques, focusing on building with available materials, creating durable and weather-resistant structures, and ensuring proper insulation and ventilation to maintain a safe and comfortable living environment.

Building with Available Materials

In a post-collapse world, the availability of modern building materials may be severely limited. As such, you will need to rely on the materials that are naturally available in your environment or that can be scavenged from abandoned buildings or other structures. The key to successful shelter construction lies in understanding the properties of these materials and how to use them effectively.

One of the most accessible materials for shelter construction is **wood**. If you are in a forested area, timber can be harvested directly from trees using basic tools like axes, saws, and wedges. Logs can be used in their raw form for building log cabins, or they can be split into planks and boards for more refined construction. Wooden shelters, such as log cabins or lean-tos, are relatively easy to construct and provide good insulation against the cold. However, wood is also flammable, so it's important to consider fire safety when using it as a primary building material.

Stone is another valuable building material, especially in areas where it is readily available. Stone structures offer excellent durability, are fireproof, and provide significant protection against the elements. Stone can be used for constructing foundations, walls, and even entire buildings. Dry-stone walling, a technique that involves stacking stones without mortar, is particularly useful for building sturdy walls and barriers. For more permanent structures, stones can be bonded with mortar, which can be made from a mixture of sand, lime, and water. Stone buildings require more labor to construct but offer superior protection and longevity.

In some regions, **earth** is the most abundant building material. Earth-based construction techniques, such as **cob**, **adobe**, and **rammed earth**, have been used for thousands of years to create durable and energy-efficient structures. **Cob** is a mixture of clay, sand, straw, and water that is shaped by hand to form thick, monolithic walls. It is particularly well-suited for moderate climates and provides excellent thermal mass, keeping interiors cool in the summer and warm in the winter. **Adobe** bricks, made from a similar mixture and dried in the sun, can be stacked to create walls that are both strong and insulating. **Rammed earth** involves compacting earth into forms to create dense, solid walls. Each of these techniques has its own advantages and can be adapted to the specific conditions of your environment.

Salvaged materials from abandoned buildings can also be invaluable in constructing your shelter. Look for items such as metal sheets, bricks, concrete blocks, windows, doors, and roofing materials that can be repurposed. Metal sheets, for example, can be used for roofing or wall panels, while bricks and concrete blocks can form the foundation or structural walls of your shelter. Scavenging requires resourcefulness and creativity, as you will need to adapt the materials you find to fit your specific needs. Additionally, scavenging should be done with caution, as collapsing structures can pose significant hazards.

Waterproofing is another critical consideration in shelter construction. Regardless of the materials you use, your shelter must be protected from water infiltration, which can cause structural damage, mold growth, and discomfort. **Thatched roofs**, made from grass, reeds, or palm fronds, are an ancient method of waterproofing and can be surprisingly effective if constructed properly. Alternatively, **tarps**, **plastic sheeting**, or **salvaged roofing materials** can be used to create a waterproof barrier. The key to effective waterproofing is ensuring that the roof has sufficient slope to allow water to run off and that all seams and joints are tightly sealed.

The foundation of your shelter is another critical aspect that will determine its stability and durability. In wet or unstable soil conditions, consider building your shelter on **stilts** or **piers** to prevent water damage and provide better air circulation underneath the structure. If the ground is stable and dry, a foundation of **stone** or **concrete blocks** can provide a solid base that will support the weight of the walls and roof. Be sure to compact the soil and level the foundation area before beginning construction to ensure that the structure remains stable over time.

In conclusion, building a shelter with available materials requires ingenuity, adaptability, and a solid understanding of the properties of those materials. Whether you are working with wood, stone, earth, or salvaged materials, the key is to choose techniques that match the resources you have on hand and the specific challenges of your environment. By mastering basic construction techniques, you can create a shelter that is not only functional and protective but also a place of refuge and comfort in a post-collapse world.

Creating Sturdy, Weather-Resistant Structures

Once you have selected your materials and begun construction, the next step is to ensure that your shelter is sturdy and weather-resistant. A well-built shelter must be able to withstand the forces of nature, including wind, rain, snow, and extreme temperatures. This requires careful attention to the construction process, from the foundation to the roof, to ensure that your shelter is both durable and secure.

The **framework** of your shelter is its skeleton and provides the necessary support for the walls and roof. In most cases, the framework will be constructed from wood or metal, which offers the strength and flexibility needed to resist the stresses of wind and weight. **Timber framing**, a traditional method that uses large wooden beams and joints to create a strong structure, is ideal for building durable shelters. The beams are connected using mortise and tenon joints, which are both strong and flexible, allowing the structure to move slightly without breaking under pressure. **Metal framing** is another option, particularly if you have access to salvaged steel or aluminum. Metal frames are fireproof, resistant to pests, and can support heavier loads than wood.

After the framework is in place, the next step is to construct the **walls**. The choice of wall material will depend on the available resources and the specific needs of your environment. **Thick walls**, made from materials such as logs, stone, or earth, provide excellent insulation and protection from the elements. They also add structural strength, helping to anchor the shelter against wind and other forces. For example, **log walls** can be stacked horizontally, with each log interlocking at the corners, creating a sturdy and weather-tight structure. **Stone walls** can be built using either dry-stone techniques or with mortar to bind the stones together, depending on the level of permanence you desire.

Insulation is a crucial component of any shelter, particularly in regions with extreme temperatures. Proper insulation keeps your shelter warm in the winter and cool in the summer, reducing the need for additional heating or cooling resources. Natural materials such as **straw**, **wool**, **cotton**, and **sheep's wool** make excellent insulators and are often readily available. These materials can be packed into walls, floors, and ceilings to create a barrier that slows the transfer of heat. Additionally, **earth** can be used as an insulator by building thick walls or burying part of the structure underground to take advantage of the earth's natural thermal mass.

The **roof** is perhaps the most critical element in creating a weather-resistant shelter. A well-constructed roof protects the interior from rain, snow, and wind, while also providing insulation. **Pitched roofs** with a steep angle are ideal for shedding water and snow, preventing buildup that can lead to leaks or structural collapse. The roofing material should be chosen based on its ability to withstand the local climate—**metal roofing**, **thatch**, **shingles**, or **tile** are all viable options, depending on what is available. Ensure that the roof is properly sealed at all joints and edges to prevent water infiltration.

Ventilation is another key factor in maintaining a comfortable and healthy living environment. A well-ventilated shelter allows for the circulation of fresh air, reducing moisture buildup and the risk of mold and mildew. **Windows**, **vents**, and **chimneys** should be strategically placed to allow air to flow through the shelter without compromising insulation or security. In colder climates, it's important to design the ventilation system so that it can be adjusted to reduce heat loss in winter while allowing for airflow in the warmer months.

To further enhance the weather resistance of your shelter, consider **applying protective coatings** to the exterior. Natural oils, such as **linseed oil** or **beeswax**, can be used to seal wood and stone, providing a water-resistant barrier that also protects against pests and rot. In addition, **paint** or **lime wash** can be applied to exterior walls to create a durable, weather-resistant surface that reflects heat and protects against moisture.

In conclusion, creating a sturdy, weather-resistant structure is essential for long-term survival in a post-collapse world. By carefully selecting materials, constructing a strong framework, and incorporating proper insulation and ventilation, you can build a shelter that will protect you from the elements and provide a safe, comfortable living space. A well-built shelter is more than just a place to sleep—it is your primary defense against the challenges of the environment and a foundation for resilience and security in uncertain times.

3.3 Advanced Building Techniques

As you move beyond the basics of shelter construction, incorporating advanced building techniques can greatly enhance the durability, sustainability, and comfort of your living space. These methods often draw from traditional practices that have been honed over centuries and are designed to make the most of local materials and environmental conditions. By integrating advanced techniques such as utilizing sustainable materials like earthbags, cob, and straw bales, incorporating renewable energy systems, and constructing communal buildings and infrastructure, you can create a shelter that not only meets your immediate survival needs but also supports long-term resilience and community building.

Utilizing Sustainable Materials: Earthbags, Cob, and Straw Bales

Sustainable materials are those that can be sourced locally and used in ways that minimize environmental impact while maximizing durability and energy efficiency. Three such materials—earthbags, cob, and straw bales—are particularly well-suited for building robust and sustainable shelters in a post-collapse world.

Earthbag construction is a versatile and highly resilient technique that involves filling sturdy bags (often made from polypropylene or burlap) with earth or other natural materials, such as sand or gravel, and stacking them to form walls. The bags are tamped down to compress the contents and create solid, load-bearing structures. This method is particularly useful in areas where wood or stone is scarce but earth is plentiful. Earthbag buildings are incredibly durable, resistant to fire, water, and pests, and provide excellent insulation due to the thermal mass of the earth. They can be shaped into domes, arches, or rectangular structures, depending on your design preferences and the local environment. Additionally, earthbag construction is labor-intensive but does not require skilled labor, making it accessible for community projects where many hands can contribute.

Cob construction is another ancient technique that uses a mixture of clay, sand, straw, and water to create monolithic walls. The mixture is applied by hand and shaped into thick, sculpted walls that are left to dry and harden. Cob buildings are known for their thermal efficiency, as the thick walls retain heat in cold weather and remain cool in the heat, reducing the need for additional energy sources. Cob is also highly sustainable, as it uses abundant and renewable materials that can often be sourced directly from the building site. Cob walls are strong and can last for centuries if properly maintained, making this technique ideal for long-term shelter construction. The aesthetic flexibility of cob allows for creative, organic designs that can include built-in furniture, sculpted details, and custom-sized windows and doors.

Straw bale construction offers a third sustainable option, particularly in areas where straw is a byproduct of local agriculture. Straw bales are stacked like bricks and secured with wooden or metal pins, then covered with plaster or clay to create thick, insulated walls. Straw bale walls are incredibly energy-efficient, providing superior insulation that keeps interiors warm in the winter and cool in the summer. This makes straw bale construction particularly valuable in regions with extreme temperatures. The plaster coating protects the straw from moisture and pests, ensuring the durability of the structure. Straw bale buildings can be constructed relatively quickly and, like cob, offer the possibility for creative design, including curved walls and large window openings. The natural materials used in straw bale construction are also biodegradable, making this an environmentally friendly building technique.

Incorporating Renewable Energy Systems

In addition to the physical construction of your shelter, incorporating renewable energy systems is crucial for ensuring long-term self-sufficiency. In a post-collapse world, reliance on traditional energy sources such as fossil fuels or grid electricity may no longer be feasible, making renewable energy a vital component of your shelter's design.

Solar energy is one of the most accessible and practical forms of renewable energy, especially in sunny regions. Photovoltaic (PV) panels can be installed on the roof or on the ground to capture sunlight and convert it into electricity, which can be used to power lights, appliances, and other essential devices. Solar water heaters can also be installed to provide hot water for bathing, cooking, and cleaning, reducing the need for fuel-based heating methods. The efficiency of solar energy systems depends on the local climate and the orientation of the panels, so it's important to assess your location's solar potential before installation.

Wind energy is another option, particularly in areas with consistent wind patterns. Small wind turbines can be installed to generate electricity, either as a primary power source or to supplement solar energy systems. Wind turbines can be mounted on rooftops or freestanding poles, and they work best in open areas where the wind is not obstructed by buildings or trees. While wind energy systems can be more complex and costly to install than solar, they provide a valuable alternative or complement to solar power, especially in regions where wind is more reliable than sunlight.

Water power can also be harnessed if your shelter is located near a flowing river or stream. Micro-hydro systems use the kinetic energy of moving water to generate electricity, providing a consistent and renewable power source. These systems are highly efficient and can produce electricity around the clock, unlike solar and wind, which are dependent on weather conditions. However, the installation of a micro-hydro system requires careful planning and engineering to ensure that it does not disrupt the local ecosystem or become damaged by seasonal fluctuations in water flow.

Constructing Communal Buildings and Infrastructure

As your survival community grows, the need for communal buildings and infrastructure will become increasingly important. These structures serve not only as functional spaces for work, storage, and gatherings but also as symbols of the community's resilience and cooperation. Constructing communal buildings requires a collaborative approach, with each member contributing their skills, labor, and resources to the project.

Community halls, **workshops**, and **storage facilities** are among the most critical communal structures. A community hall provides a central meeting place where members can gather for discussions, decision-making, and social events. This building should be large enough to accommodate the entire community and should be constructed with durability and comfort in mind. Workshops are essential for maintaining tools, producing goods, and carrying out repairs. These spaces should be equipped with workbenches, storage for tools and materials, and adequate ventilation and lighting. Storage facilities, such as barns or warehouses, are necessary for storing food, supplies, and equipment. These buildings should be secure, well-ventilated, and protected from pests and weather.

Infrastructure development is also crucial for supporting the needs of the community. This includes creating roads and pathways for easy access to different parts of the community, digging wells or installing water systems for a reliable water supply, and constructing waste management systems such as composting toilets or septic tanks. Building and maintaining this infrastructure requires careful planning and ongoing maintenance to ensure that it meets the community's needs without causing environmental degradation.

In conclusion, advanced building techniques offer a pathway to creating durable, sustainable, and resilient shelters that can support not only individual survival but also the development of a thriving community. By utilizing sustainable materials, incorporating renewable energy systems, and constructing communal buildings and infrastructure, you can create a living environment that is not only functional and protective but also capable of supporting long-term growth and stability in a post-collapse world. These techniques, rooted in both traditional wisdom and modern innovation, provide the tools needed to build a future where self-sufficiency and community resilience are the foundations of survival.

3.4 Maintenance and Repairs

Constructing a sturdy and sustainable shelter is only the first step in ensuring long-term survival and comfort in a post-collapse world. Just as important is the ongoing maintenance and repair of your shelter, which will ensure that it continues to provide protection against the elements, security from potential threats, and a comfortable living environment. Without regular upkeep, even the most well-built structure will eventually deteriorate, leading to potentially life-threatening vulnerabilities. This section will explore the importance of regular inspection routines, common issues you may encounter, DIY repair techniques, and strategies for upgrading your shelter over time.

Regular Inspection Routines

The foundation of effective maintenance is regular inspection. A systematic approach to inspecting your shelter allows you to identify and address potential problems before they escalate into serious issues. Inspections should be conducted seasonally, at a minimum, and ideally after any significant weather events, such as storms, heavy rains, or extreme temperatures, that could impact the integrity of your shelter.

Begin each inspection by evaluating the **roof** of your shelter. The roof is your primary defense against the elements, and any damage or wear can lead to leaks, water damage, and structural instability. Check for missing or damaged shingles, tiles, or other roofing materials. If your roof is made of thatch or metal, look for signs of wear, rust, or degradation. Pay close attention to the areas around chimneys, vents, and skylights, as these are common points of entry for water. Clear any debris, such as leaves or branches, that may have accumulated, as this can trap moisture and accelerate deterioration.

Next, examine the **walls** of your shelter, both inside and out. Look for cracks, holes, or gaps in the structure that could allow water, wind, or pests to enter. In particular, check the areas around windows and doors, where the sealant or caulking may have degraded over time. If your walls are made of wood, inspect for signs of rot, insect damage, or warping. For stone or earth walls, check for any loose or crumbling sections that may need reinforcement. On the interior, be on the lookout for signs of mold, mildew, or dampness, which could indicate a leak or poor ventilation.

The **foundation** is another critical area to inspect. A strong foundation is essential for the stability of your shelter, and any issues here can quickly lead to more serious structural problems. Look for cracks in the foundation, uneven settling, or any signs of erosion or water pooling around the base of your shelter. If your shelter is built on stilts or piers, check for signs of wood rot or weakening in the supports.

Finally, don't overlook the **doors and windows**. These are not only points of entry for people but also for air, water, and pests. Ensure that all doors and windows open and close properly, that the seals are intact, and that there are no gaps or cracks around the frames. Locks and latches should be functional and secure, providing adequate protection against intruders.

Common Issues and DIY Repair Techniques

Even with regular maintenance, issues will inevitably arise that require attention. Being prepared with the knowledge and tools to handle common repairs can save time, resources, and potentially prevent larger problems.

Leaks and water damage are among the most common issues in any shelter. If you notice water stains on the ceiling or walls, act quickly to locate and repair the source of the leak. For small leaks in the roof, applying roofing cement or sealant to the affected area may be sufficient. For larger issues, you may need to replace damaged shingles or sections of the roof entirely. Inside the shelter, remove any damaged materials, such as drywall or insulation, that have been compromised by water, and ensure the area is thoroughly dried before making repairs to prevent mold growth.

Rot and insect damage in wood structures are also common, particularly in damp or humid environments. If you identify rot, cut out the affected section and replace it with new wood, treating the area with a preservative to prevent further decay. For insect damage, such as from termites or carpenter ants, it's important to eliminate the source of the infestation and treat the wood with insecticides or natural deterrents, like borax, to protect the structure.

Cracks in walls or foundations can be a sign of settling or shifting in your shelter. Small cracks can often be filled with mortar or caulk to prevent them from widening. However, larger cracks may indicate a more serious structural issue that requires reinforcement, such as adding support beams or underpinning the foundation. In earth-based structures, like cob or adobe, cracks can often be repaired by reapplying the original mixture and blending it into the surrounding wall.

Pest infestations are another challenge that can compromise the integrity of your shelter. Rodents, insects, and other pests can cause significant damage if left unchecked. Regularly inspect your shelter for signs of pests, such as droppings, nests, or gnaw marks. Seal any potential entry points, such as gaps in walls or around doors and windows, and consider setting traps or using natural repellents, like peppermint oil or diatomaceous earth, to deter pests.

Strategies for Upgrading Your Shelter Over Time

As your shelter ages and your needs evolve, it may be necessary to upgrade or enhance your living space. These upgrades can range from improving insulation and energy efficiency to expanding the size of your shelter to accommodate more people or activities.

One of the most impactful upgrades you can make is improving **insulation**. As mentioned earlier, natural materials like straw, wool, or earth can provide excellent insulation, but as resources allow, you may consider adding modern insulation materials, such as foam boards or reflective barriers, to further improve your shelter's thermal performance. Proper insulation not only makes your shelter more comfortable but also reduces the amount of fuel needed for heating and cooling, which is crucial in a resource-scarce environment.

Another upgrade to consider is the addition of **renewable energy systems**, such as solar panels, wind turbines, or micro-hydro generators. These systems can provide reliable electricity for lighting, heating, and powering essential devices, making your shelter more self-sufficient and less reliant on external resources. Even small-scale systems can make a significant difference in your daily life and contribute to the long-term sustainability of your shelter.

Expanding your shelter may become necessary as your community grows or as you accumulate more supplies and equipment. When planning an expansion, ensure that any additions are structurally sound and integrated with the existing shelter. Consider how the expansion will impact the overall layout and functionality of your living space, and plan for additional insulation, ventilation, and waterproofing as needed.

Finally, **modernizing infrastructure** within your shelter, such as improving water collection and filtration systems, upgrading waste management solutions, or enhancing food storage capabilities, can greatly increase the efficiency and comfort of your living space. These upgrades not only improve your quality of life but also help to future-proof your shelter against changing conditions and needs.

In conclusion, regular maintenance and repairs are essential for the long-term viability of your shelter. By establishing consistent inspection routines, addressing common issues promptly, and strategically upgrading your shelter over time, you can ensure that your living space remains safe, secure, and comfortable in the face of an uncertain future. The effort you invest in maintaining and improving your shelter will pay off in increased resilience, security, and sustainability for years to come.

Chapter 4: Water Management and Sanitation

Water is life, and proper sanitation is critical for health. This chapter provides practical solutions for managing water resources and maintaining hygiene, crucial for preventing disease and ensuring a healthy community.

4.1 Finding and Purifying Water

In any scenario where civilization has collapsed or resources are scarce, access to clean and safe water becomes paramount. Water is not just a basic necessity; it is the foundation upon which survival hinges. Understanding where to locate water sources and how to purify them is essential knowledge that every individual must possess when rebuilding or maintaining a community.

When you find yourself in the wild or in an environment where established water systems are no longer functional, the first step is to locate a viable water source. Streams, rivers, lakes, and even dew on plants can be potential sources of water. In arid regions, look for natural depressions where water might collect after rainfall or dig near dry riverbeds, which can often reveal water just below the surface. Additionally, certain plants, such as bamboo or the base of cacti, can be tapped for water. However, these methods require knowledge and practice, and it's essential to understand that not all water sources are safe to drink directly.

Once you've located water, the next critical step is purification. Even seemingly clean water can harbor pathogens that cause life-threatening diseases. The most reliable method of water purification is boiling. Bringing water to a rolling boil for at least one minute (and three minutes at higher altitudes) kills most bacteria, viruses, and parasites. However, boiling requires a heat source and a container, which might not always be available. In such cases, filtration becomes a practical alternative.

There are several filtration methods, ranging from basic DIY systems to more sophisticated portable filters. A simple yet effective method involves using a cloth to filter out large particles followed by a homemade filter using layers of sand, charcoal, and gravel in a container to remove smaller contaminants. Commercial portable water filters, which are lightweight and designed for emergency situations, can remove up to 99.9% of pathogens. Another method is chemical treatment using iodine tablets or chlorine drops, which can effectively neutralize harmful microorganisms. However, these chemicals may leave an unpleasant taste and are less effective against certain parasites.

In addition to purification, setting up a rainwater collection system can provide a consistent and renewable water supply, especially in regions with regular rainfall. This system can be as simple as placing containers under natural runoff points or constructing a more complex setup with gutters, pipes, and storage tanks. Rainwater, although generally safer than ground or surface water, still requires filtration and possibly chemical treatment to ensure it is safe for consumption. By mastering these techniques, you not only secure a vital resource but also gain resilience in the face of potential future crises.

4.2. Building Water Systems

Beyond finding and purifying water, the next step in ensuring long-term survival is constructing a reliable water system that can sustainably supply your needs. Building wells, cisterns, and gravity-fed systems are foundational projects that ensure a stable water supply for drinking, agriculture, and sanitation.

Constructing a well is one of the most effective ways to access groundwater, which is often less contaminated than surface water. Depending on the depth of the water table, wells can be hand-dug or drilled. Hand-dug wells are more labor-intensive but can be a viable option in areas where the water table is shallow. The process involves digging a wide shaft and lining it with stones, bricks, or concrete to prevent collapse and contamination. For deeper water tables, drilling is necessary, which requires specialized equipment to bore a narrow hole deep into the ground. It's crucial to protect the well from surface contamination by constructing a sturdy cover and ensuring the surrounding area is kept clean.

Cisterns, on the other hand, are storage systems designed to collect and store rainwater or surface runoff. These can be built above or below ground and are usually made from concrete, stone, or modern materials like plastic. The key to an effective cistern is ensuring it is sealed to prevent contamination and that it includes a filtration system to clean the water before it is used. Cisterns can provide a crucial backup supply during dry periods when other water sources may not be available.

Designing a gravity-fed water system is another critical skill, particularly for agricultural purposes or supplying water to a community. Gravity-fed systems use the natural slope of the land to move water from a higher elevation to where it is needed, eliminating the need for pumps. This system involves setting up a reservoir at a higher elevation and using pipes or channels to direct the water downhill. These systems are energy-efficient and can be used for irrigation, providing a steady flow of water to crops, or even for supplying water to homes if the topography allows.

Understanding and implementing these water systems not only secures a reliable water supply but also supports the broader goal of sustainability. These methods are designed to be low-maintenance and rely on readily available materials, making them accessible even in a resource-constrained environment. By establishing such systems, you lay the groundwork for a resilient community capable of thriving independently of external resources.

4.3 Waste Management and Sanitation

The importance of waste management and sanitation in a post-collapse environment cannot be overstated. In scenarios where modern plumbing and waste disposal systems have ceased to function, communities must adopt sustainable practices to manage human waste and other refuse. Poor sanitation is one of the quickest routes to the outbreak of diseases such as cholera, dysentery, and typhoid, which can spread rapidly in crowded, resource-limited settings. Therefore, implementing effective waste management and sanitation systems is not just a matter of maintaining comfort but is essential for preserving the health and well-being of the community.

One of the most practical solutions for managing human waste in a grid-down scenario is the use of composting toilets. Unlike conventional flush toilets, composting toilets do not require a continuous supply of water, making them ideal for off-grid living. These systems operate by separating liquid and solid waste, with the latter being broken down by aerobic bacteria into a stable, non-toxic compost. Constructing a composting toilet can be done with basic materials: a sturdy wooden structure for privacy, a collection chamber for waste, and a ventilation system to minimize odors and facilitate aerobic decomposition. The use of carbon-rich materials such as sawdust, straw, or dry leaves is critical in balancing the nitrogen content of human waste, thus accelerating the composting process and preventing foul smells.

The compost produced by these toilets can, after sufficient decomposition, be safely used to enrich soil for non-edible plants or even for edible crops in some cases, provided it is adequately processed. This approach not only addresses waste disposal but also contributes to the sustainability of the community by closing the nutrient loop and enhancing soil fertility. However, it is crucial to follow best practices in compost management, such as ensuring the composting process reaches temperatures high enough to kill pathogens, and allowing the compost to cure for several months before use. This not only ensures safety but also maximizes the nutrient value of the compost.

Beyond human waste, managing greywater—water that comes from sinks, showers, and laundry—plays a vital role in maintaining hygiene and preventing environmental contamination. Unlike blackwater, greywater contains fewer pathogens and can be treated and reused for irrigation or flushing toilets. Designing a greywater system requires careful planning to avoid contamination and ensure that the water is safely reused. Simple greywater systems can involve diverting water through a gravel and sand filter, where it can be further purified by plants in a constructed wetland or mulch basin. These natural filtration systems are highly effective and sustainable, requiring minimal maintenance while providing essential irrigation for gardens or agricultural areas.

More advanced greywater systems can include multiple stages of filtration and treatment, such as using biochar or activated carbon to remove chemical contaminants, or employing aerobic treatment units to further break down organic matter. These systems are scalable depending on the size of the community and the available resources. By effectively treating and reusing greywater, a community can significantly reduce its demand for fresh water, making it a critical component of any water management strategy in a resource-constrained environment.

Additionally, the prevention of contamination is paramount in any waste management and sanitation strategy. This involves not only the proper construction and placement of latrines and composting systems but also the education and enforcement of strict hygiene practices. Latrines should be located at least 200 feet away from water sources and on lower ground to prevent runoff from contaminating the community's water supply. Regular handwashing, particularly after using the toilet and before handling food, should be rigorously enforced. In a situation where medical facilities may be limited or non-existent, preventing the spread of disease through proper waste management and sanitation is crucial for the survival of the community.

Moreover, communities must establish protocols for the disposal of non-organic waste, such as plastics and metals, which can accumulate and pose environmental hazards. In the absence of formal waste disposal systems, recycling and reusing materials becomes not only a practical solution but a necessity. Scrap metals can be repurposed for tools and construction, while plastics can be used for insulation or waterproofing. Organic waste, aside from human excrement, can be composted to create additional fertilizer for crops, further enhancing the sustainability of the community.

In conclusion, waste management and sanitation are not merely logistical concerns but are fundamental to the survival and health of a post-collapse society. Through the use of composting toilets, greywater systems, and strict hygiene practices, communities can mitigate the risks associated with poor sanitation, prevent the outbreak of disease, and create a sustainable environment that supports long-term survival and growth. These practices, while simple, require diligent implementation and maintenance to ensure their effectiveness, making them a critical component of any survival strategy.

4.4 Community Water Infrastructure

As the scale of survival efforts increases from individuals and small groups to larger communities, the complexity and importance of water management grow exponentially. Building and maintaining a robust community water infrastructure is crucial not only for ensuring access to safe drinking water but also for supporting agricultural activities, sanitation, and overall public health. A well-designed water infrastructure enables a community to thrive even in the most challenging circumstances, making it a foundational element of any long-term survival plan.

The first step in developing community water infrastructure is a comprehensive assessment of the community's water needs and available resources. This includes identifying potential water sources, such as rivers, lakes, underground aquifers, or rainwater, and determining their capacity to meet the community's needs. It is essential to consider both current and future water demands, accounting for population growth, agricultural expansion, and seasonal variations in water availability. This assessment should also include an evaluation of the local geography and climate, which will influence the design and placement of water infrastructure.

Once the assessment is complete, the next phase involves designing a water distribution system that ensures equitable access to all members of the community. This system might include a combination of wells, cisterns, reservoirs, and pipelines. For instance, a central reservoir can be constructed to store water from multiple sources, which is then distributed through a network of gravity-fed pipelines to various parts of the community. Gravity-fed systems are particularly advantageous in off-grid scenarios because they require no external power source, relying instead on the natural gradient of the land to move water from higher to lower elevations. These systems are not only efficient but also relatively easy to maintain, making them ideal for long-term use.

In addition to ensuring equitable distribution, it is crucial to establish protocols for the sustainable use and management of water resources. This includes implementing water-saving techniques, such as drip irrigation for agriculture, which minimizes water loss due to evaporation and runoff. Communities should also prioritize the protection of water sources from contamination. This can be achieved by designating protected areas around wells and reservoirs, preventing the use of harmful chemicals in nearby agricultural practices, and educating the community about the importance of safeguarding their water supply.

Maintaining the infrastructure is another critical aspect of community water management. This involves regular inspections of wells, pipelines, and storage tanks to detect and repair leaks or other damage promptly. In a post-collapse scenario, where access to materials and skilled labor may be limited, it is vital to train members of the community in basic maintenance and repair techniques. By creating a team responsible for the upkeep of water infrastructure, communities can ensure that their water supply remains reliable and safe over the long term.

Furthermore, community involvement in water management is essential for the success of these systems. Establishing a water committee or cooperative can help manage the distribution of water, resolve disputes, and coordinate maintenance efforts. Such a committee should represent all sectors of the community, ensuring that the needs and concerns of all members are addressed. In times of scarcity, these committees can also implement rationing systems to ensure that water is distributed fairly and that essential needs, such as drinking and sanitation, are prioritized.

Lastly, communities must prepare for emergencies, such as droughts or contamination incidents, that could disrupt the water supply. This requires having contingency plans in place, such as alternative water sources, emergency storage tanks, and purification methods. Communities might also invest in technologies that allow for the rapid deployment of additional water resources, such as portable desalination units or mobile water purification systems. In addition, stockpiling water purification tablets and training community members in their use can provide a crucial backup in the event of an emergency.

In conclusion, building a community water infrastructure is a complex but essential task that requires careful planning, sustainable management, and ongoing maintenance. By ensuring that all members of the community have access to clean, safe water, and by preparing for potential disruptions, communities can build resilience and increase their chances of survival in the long term. Water is the lifeblood of any society, and in a post-collapse world, it will be the cornerstone upon which a new civilization is built. The successful management of this resource will not only sustain life but will also enable communities to thrive and grow, even in the most challenging environments.

Chapter 5: Reestablishing Communication and Transportation

Reconnecting with others is essential in a post-collapse world. This chapter outlines how to rebuild communication and transportation networks, enabling you to stay connected, share resources, and coordinate efforts with neighboring communities.

5.1 Emergency Communication Systems

In the aftermath of a societal collapse or disaster, one of the most critical challenges communities face is the loss of reliable communication systems. The ability to communicate effectively, both within a community and with the outside world, is essential for coordinating relief efforts, ensuring safety, and sharing vital information. As modern communication networks—such as the internet, mobile phones, and landlines—fail, it becomes imperative to revert to more basic, yet reliable, methods of communication. Reestablishing these systems quickly and efficiently can mean the difference between chaos and order in the crucial early stages of recovery.

One of the most practical and accessible forms of emergency communication is the use of radio. Basic radio operation and maintenance skills are invaluable in a grid-down scenario. Hand-crank or battery-operated radios, such as those using shortwave or HAM frequencies, can be used to receive critical information from outside the immediate area, including weather updates, news from other communities, and emergency broadcasts. Learning to operate a radio is relatively straightforward, but it requires practice and familiarity with the equipment. Key skills include tuning to the correct frequencies, understanding radio etiquette, and maintaining the equipment in working order, including regular checks on batteries and antennas.

In addition to receiving information, communities need to establish a local communication network. This can be achieved by distributing handheld radios to key members of the community, such as leaders, security personnel, and medical teams. These radios can operate on a shared frequency, allowing for real-time communication across distances that might otherwise be difficult to traverse quickly. Establishing a communication schedule or protocol ensures that the network remains organized and that critical messages are relayed efficiently. In a scenario where privacy is a concern, using coded language or agreed-upon phrases can protect sensitive information from being intercepted by others.

Another crucial aspect of emergency communication is the use of non-verbal methods, such as Morse code, which can be transmitted via light, sound, or radio. Morse code is a simple yet effective way to communicate when voice transmission is not possible, either due to distance, noise, or the need for secrecy. Learning the basics of Morse code is relatively easy, and it can be an invaluable tool in a survival situation. For instance, tapping out messages on a metal surface, flashing a light in a specific pattern, or sending short radio pulses can all convey information discreetly and over long distances. Communities can establish a standard for Morse code usage, ensuring that everyone is familiar with the common codes and signals.

Beyond Morse code, other non-verbal communication methods include using signal flags, hand signals, and written messages. Signal flags, for example, can be used to communicate over short distances, especially in open areas where visibility is clear. Hand signals can be crucial in situations where silence is necessary, such as during security operations or hunting. Written messages, although slower, can be used for detailed instructions or when communicating with someone in a different location within the community. These messages can be delivered by trusted individuals or left in predetermined locations for pickup, ensuring that even in the absence of real-time communication, information can still be shared effectively.

In a survival scenario, redundancy in communication systems is vital. By integrating multiple methods—radio, Morse code, signal flags, and hand signals—communities can ensure that they remain connected even if one system fails. The key to successful communication lies in planning, training, and regular practice. Communities should conduct drills to ensure that all members are familiar with the equipment and protocols, and that they can operate effectively under stress. By establishing a robust emergency communication system, communities not only enhance their resilience but also improve their ability to coordinate efforts, share resources, and protect their members in times of crisis.

5.2 Rebuilding Transportation Networks

Transportation is another cornerstone of survival and recovery in a post-collapse environment. As the intricate networks of highways, railways, and public transit systems become compromised or entirely non-functional, the ability to move people, goods, and resources within and between communities becomes a significant challenge. Rebuilding transportation networks is crucial for ensuring the continued flow of essential supplies, enabling medical aid, facilitating communication, and supporting the overall mobility of the population. In the absence of modern vehicles and infrastructure, communities must adopt alternative transportation methods and maintain their roadways to sustain their daily operations and long-term recovery.

The first step in rebuilding transportation networks is clearing and maintaining existing roads. In many cases, roadways may be obstructed by debris, overgrown vegetation, or damage from natural disasters. Clearing these roads is a labor-intensive task but one that is essential for restoring basic transportation. Communities should organize work crews to systematically clear major routes, starting with those that connect essential locations such as food storage areas, medical facilities, and water sources. This might involve removing fallen trees, repairing potholes, and reinforcing vulnerable sections of the road to prevent further deterioration. Simple tools such as shovels, axes, and wheelbarrows can be invaluable in these efforts, though heavier equipment, if available, can greatly expedite the process.

Once the roads are cleared, it's important to establish a routine for their maintenance. Without regular upkeep, even cleared roads can quickly become impassable again, especially in areas prone to flooding or landslides. Communities should designate individuals or teams responsible for inspecting the roads regularly and carrying out necessary repairs. In addition to physical labor, basic engineering knowledge can be helpful in maintaining infrastructure, such as understanding drainage patterns to prevent water damage or knowing how to reinforce a bridge or culvert. In the absence of advanced materials, creative use of available resources, such as using stones or logs to reinforce roadbeds, can make a significant difference in the longevity of these transportation networks.

In parallel with road maintenance, alternative transportation methods must be developed to adapt to the limitations of a post-collapse environment. With fuel supplies likely to be scarce or unavailable, reliance on motor vehicles will diminish. Bicycles, for instance, become an invaluable mode of transportation due to their efficiency, ease of maintenance, and ability to traverse a variety of terrains. Communities should encourage the use of bicycles for short to medium-distance travel and establish repair stations where individuals can maintain and fix their bikes using scavenged parts or simple tools. Training workshops on basic bicycle maintenance, such as fixing a flat tire or adjusting brakes, can empower community members to keep their bicycles in working order.

In addition to bicycles, carts and wagons drawn by humans or animals offer a practical solution for transporting heavier loads, such as food supplies, building materials, or water. Communities can build or repurpose carts using wood, metal, and other salvaged materials. These carts can be designed for specific purposes, such as mobile water tanks or supply wagons, and can be pulled by hand or by animals such as horses, donkeys, or oxen if available. Establishing designated routes for these carts helps to streamline transportation within the community, reducing congestion and ensuring that goods are delivered efficiently.

Another aspect of rebuilding transportation networks involves setting up a community transport system. In larger communities or those spread out over a wide area, organizing a system where people and goods can be transported regularly is essential. This might involve scheduling regular trips between key locations, such as market areas, medical centers, and communal kitchens. Volunteers or designated transport coordinators can manage this system, ensuring that everyone has access to the resources they need. For longer distances or rougher terrain, innovative solutions such as constructing simple rail carts on abandoned railway tracks, or even utilizing waterways where possible, can extend the community's transportation capabilities.

Finally, rebuilding transportation networks isn't just about physical infrastructure but also about reestablishing the social and logistical systems that keep a community moving. This includes organizing work groups, coordinating the distribution of resources, and ensuring that everyone understands their role in maintaining and using the transportation systems. Clear communication and cooperation are key to these efforts. Regular meetings or community assemblies can be used to discuss transportation needs, address challenges, and plan for future expansions or repairs.

In summary, rebuilding transportation networks in a post-collapse world requires a combination of physical labor, creative problem-solving, and community cooperation. By clearing and maintaining roads, adopting alternative transportation methods, and setting up a coordinated transport system, communities can ensure that people and goods continue to move efficiently, supporting both immediate survival and long-term recovery efforts. These efforts lay the groundwork for a resilient, self-sustaining community capable of adapting to the challenges of a changed world.

5.3 Signaling for Help

In the wake of a disaster or collapse, one of the immediate concerns is the ability to signal for help, especially when cut off from conventional communication networks. Effective signaling can attract rescuers, alert nearby communities, or coordinate efforts within a group. The ability to create and use both visual and auditory signals is a crucial survival skill that can make the difference between being isolated and receiving timely assistance. Mastering these techniques requires an understanding of the environment, the available resources, and the context in which the signals will be used.

Visual signals are among the most effective ways to communicate over long distances, particularly when there is a clear line of sight. Signal fires are one of the oldest and most reliable methods for attracting attention. To create an effective signal fire, location is key—elevated areas such as hilltops or clearings offer the best visibility. The fire itself should be built large and hot to produce thick smoke that can be seen from far away. Using green vegetation, rubber, or oil can enhance the amount of smoke, making the signal more visible during the day. For nighttime signaling, keeping a stockpile of dry wood or other flammable materials ensures the fire burns brightly. Arranging the fires in patterns—such as three fires in a triangular formation or a straight line—can indicate distress, which is universally recognized as a call for help. It's also important to maintain the fire continuously until help arrives or other communication methods are established.

In addition to signal fires, other visual signaling methods include the use of mirrors, flares, and brightly colored fabrics or flags. Mirrors can reflect sunlight over vast distances, creating flashes of light that are visible to aircraft, ships, or distant observers. The technique involves angling the mirror to catch sunlight and directing the reflected beam towards the intended target. This method requires clear skies and direct sunlight but is highly effective during daylight hours. Flares are another potent signaling tool, often used in maritime settings but equally useful on land. They produce bright light and sometimes smoke, drawing attention from miles away. However, flares have a limited duration and should be used strategically, perhaps in conjunction with ongoing visual signals like fires or flags.

Flags or pieces of brightly colored fabric can serve as improvised signal devices when placed in open, visible areas or waved to attract attention. The international distress signal of waving a flag or any visible object overhead is a simple yet effective way to signal distress. In snow-covered or desert environments, using materials that contrast sharply with the surroundings increases the visibility of your signal. Additionally, arranging rocks, logs, or any available materials in large, distinct shapes such as "SOS" or an arrow pointing in a particular direction can communicate specific messages to rescuers from the air.

Auditory signals complement visual signals, particularly in environments where visibility is limited or during nighttime. Whistles, horns, or makeshift sound devices like banging on metal objects can carry over long distances, particularly in open spaces or across water. The international distress signal for sound is three short bursts followed by three long bursts, then three short bursts again, repeated at intervals. This pattern is recognized globally as a call for help. In scenarios where a whistle or horn is unavailable, human voice signals like shouting or yelling in a specific rhythm can also be used, though these are less effective over long distances or in noisy environments.

The use of signal devices should be paired with an understanding of the context in which they are deployed. For instance, signaling in a densely wooded area may require a combination of loud sounds to penetrate the forest canopy and bright light sources like flares or fires to pierce through the shadows. In mountainous regions, echoes and reflections can distort sound, so visual signals may take precedence. Additionally, when signaling from a vehicle or building, using reflective surfaces or flashing lights can attract attention more effectively than sound alone.

Maintaining signals consistently over time is crucial, particularly in rescue scenarios where the arrival of help might take hours or even days. Having a plan for replenishing signal materials—such as additional firewood for signal fires or spare batteries for electronic devices—ensures that the signals can be sustained. Communities should designate individuals or teams responsible for monitoring and maintaining the signals, ensuring that they are kept active until help arrives. Regular training and drills on signal use can prepare community members to respond quickly and efficiently in an emergency, reducing panic and increasing the likelihood of successful rescue.

In summary, signaling for help involves more than just knowing how to start a fire or blow a whistle; it requires strategic thinking, environmental awareness, and the ability to sustain efforts over time. By mastering both visual and auditory signaling techniques, communities can enhance their chances of being found and assisted in the event of an emergency. These skills are essential not only for individual survival but also for the broader safety and cohesion of the community as it navigates the challenges of a post-collapse environment.

5.4 Long-Distance Travel and Exploration

As communities stabilize in the aftermath of a disaster or collapse, the need for long-distance travel and exploration becomes increasingly important. Whether for the purpose of scouting new resources, establishing connections with other communities, or simply mapping out the surrounding terrain, the ability to travel efficiently and safely over long distances is a critical skill. However, without modern technology like GPS or vehicles, long-distance travel poses significant challenges, requiring careful planning, physical endurance, and a deep understanding of traditional navigation techniques.

The first step in preparing for long-distance travel is thorough planning. This involves not only selecting the destination but also considering the safest and most efficient route to get there. Factors such as terrain, weather conditions, and potential hazards must be taken into account. For example, traveling through dense forests or mountainous areas requires different preparations compared to journeys across open plains or deserts. In addition to mapping out the route, it's essential to identify potential rest stops, water sources, and safe shelters along the way. Understanding the natural environment is crucial—knowing where to find edible plants, water, and safe resting places can make the difference between a successful journey and a dangerous ordeal.

Without the aid of modern navigational tools, travelers must rely on traditional techniques such as the use of maps, compasses, and natural landmarks. Creating a simple map of the area, even if it's just a rough sketch, provides a visual reference that can help travelers stay oriented. Compasses, which point to magnetic north, are invaluable for maintaining a consistent direction, especially in environments where landmarks are scarce. However, it's also important to know how to navigate without a compass. Natural indicators like the position of the sun and stars, the growth patterns of moss on trees, and the flow of rivers can all serve as guides. For instance, in the Northern Hemisphere, the North Star (Polaris) is a reliable indicator of true north at night, while the sun's position in the sky can help determine cardinal directions during the day.

Building simple maps based on exploration and shared knowledge can help future expeditions and provide a foundation for understanding the larger environment. As travelers explore new areas, they can add details to these maps, such as noting the locations of water sources, fertile lands, and dangerous areas. Over time, these maps can evolve into more comprehensive documents that benefit the entire community, aiding in resource management, defense, and future expansion. Map-making also fosters a sense of collaboration, as different explorers contribute their findings, leading to a more nuanced understanding of the surrounding region.

Physical preparation is just as important as planning and navigation skills. Long-distance travel is physically demanding, particularly in rough or unfamiliar terrain. Travelers must be in good physical condition, capable of walking long distances while carrying supplies. Endurance training, such as regular hiking with a loaded backpack, can help build the necessary stamina. It's also important to pack wisely, carrying only essential items to avoid being weighed down. A well-prepared traveler's pack might include food, water, a first-aid kit, tools for making fire and shelter, and a basic navigation kit (such as a compass, map, and signaling devices). Lightweight, durable clothing that can protect against the elements is also crucial, as is sturdy footwear designed for the terrain.

Long-distance travel also involves psychological challenges. The isolation and uncertainty of traveling through unfamiliar territory can be daunting, particularly in a post-collapse world where dangers are ever-present. Mental resilience is key to overcoming these challenges. Travelers must be prepared to face setbacks, such as adverse weather, injuries, or unexpected obstacles, with calmness and adaptability. Having a clear purpose for the journey—whether it's to find a new water source, establish contact with another community, or explore potential agricultural land—helps maintain focus and motivation, even in difficult conditions.

Finally, successful long-distance travel requires a strong emphasis on safety and risk management. Traveling in groups is generally safer than traveling alone, as it provides mutual support and protection against threats. Groups can share the burden of carrying supplies, watch out for each other's well-being, and respond more effectively to emergencies. Establishing clear communication protocols, such as designated meeting points and signals for distress, further enhances safety. In the event that a traveler becomes separated from the group, having a prearranged plan for reuniting can prevent panic and ensure that the journey continues smoothly.

In conclusion, long-distance travel and exploration are vital for the expansion and sustainability of a post-collapse community. These endeavors require careful planning, physical and mental preparation, and a deep understanding of traditional navigation methods. By mastering these skills, communities can explore new territories, forge connections with other groups, and secure the resources necessary for long-term survival. As communities begin to rebuild and expand, the ability to navigate and explore the surrounding world will become increasingly important, laying the groundwork for a new era of discovery and growth.

Chapter 6: Power and Energy Solutions

Energy powers progress. In this chapter, discover how to harness renewable energy sources and develop sustainable power systems that support the needs of your community and reduce dependence on finite resources.

6.1. Harnessing Solar Energy

In the quest to rebuild a self-sufficient society, harnessing solar energy is one of the most practical and sustainable solutions available. Solar energy, abundant and renewable, offers a reliable source of power that can be used for a variety of essential tasks, from heating water to cooking food. The technology to capture and utilize solar energy has advanced significantly, making it accessible even in a post-collapse scenario. By understanding how to build, maintain, and effectively utilize solar systems, communities can reduce their reliance on finite resources and create a more resilient energy infrastructure.

One of the most effective ways to harness solar energy is through the use of solar panels, which convert sunlight into electricity. Building and maintaining solar panels may seem daunting, but with the right materials and knowledge, it is a manageable task. Solar panels are typically made from photovoltaic (PV) cells that are capable of converting sunlight into direct current (DC) electricity. While manufacturing PV cells from scratch requires advanced technology, scavenging existing solar panels from abandoned buildings or repurposing damaged ones can be a viable option. Repairing and reassembling these panels requires understanding basic electrical concepts, such as wiring, soldering, and voltage regulation. Once assembled, the panels must be positioned optimally—typically at a 30-degree angle facing south in the Northern Hemisphere—to maximize exposure to sunlight throughout the day.

In addition to building and maintaining the panels themselves, it is crucial to integrate them into a functioning electrical system. This includes setting up an inverter to convert the DC electricity generated by the solar panels into alternating current (AC), which is used by most household appliances. Battery storage systems are also essential for storing excess energy generated during sunny periods, which can then be used during cloudy days or at night. Regular maintenance, such as cleaning the panels to remove dust and debris and checking connections for wear, ensures that the system continues to operate efficiently. By mastering these skills, communities can create a sustainable and reliable source of electricity that is independent of external power grids.

Beyond electricity generation, solar energy can also be harnessed for heating water, a critical need in both household and agricultural contexts. Solar water heaters use the sun's energy to heat water directly, offering a simple yet effective way to provide hot water without consuming electricity or fuel. There are various designs for solar water heaters, ranging from simple batch systems that heat water in an insulated tank exposed to the sun, to more complex systems that circulate water through solar collectors and then store it in a separate insulated tank. Building a solar water heater requires materials like black-painted metal pipes, which absorb heat, and glass or clear plastic covers, which create a greenhouse effect to trap the heat. By understanding the principles of thermal mass and heat transfer, one can design and construct a solar water heater that meets the needs of a household or community, reducing the reliance on traditional water heating methods.

Solar energy can also be harnessed for cooking and food preservation through the use of solar cookers and dehydrators. Solar cookers use reflective surfaces, such as aluminum foil or mirrors, to concentrate sunlight onto a cooking pot or surface, generating enough heat to cook food. These cookers can be constructed from simple materials like cardboard, glass, and reflective foil, making them accessible even in resource-scarce environments. Solar cookers are particularly useful in areas where fuel is scarce or expensive, as they eliminate the need for wood, gas, or electricity to prepare meals. Similarly, solar dehydrators use the sun's heat to dry fruits, vegetables, and meat, preserving them for long-term storage. A basic solar dehydrator can be built using a wooden frame, mesh trays for the food, and a glass or plastic cover to trap heat. Proper ventilation is key to ensuring that moisture is efficiently removed from the food, preventing spoilage.

By harnessing solar energy through these various methods, communities can significantly enhance their energy independence and sustainability. Solar panels, water heaters, cookers, and dehydrators not only provide practical solutions for daily needs but also contribute to the overall resilience of the community by reducing dependence on external energy sources. As the sun's energy is free and abundant, mastering the techniques to capture and use it effectively is a crucial step toward rebuilding a self-sufficient and sustainable society.

6.2 Wind and Water Power

While solar energy is a versatile and widely applicable solution, it is not always reliable, especially in regions with limited sunlight. In such cases, harnessing the power of wind and water can provide essential energy alternatives. Wind and water power have been used for centuries to perform tasks such as grinding grain, pumping water, and generating electricity. By constructing and utilizing wind turbines and water wheels, communities can tap into these natural forces to generate power, ensuring a more diverse and stable energy supply. Integrating wind and water energy into the community's energy grid can enhance resilience and sustainability, especially when combined with solar power.

Wind turbines are one of the most effective ways to generate electricity from wind. A wind turbine works by converting the kinetic energy of the wind into mechanical energy, which is then converted into electrical energy through a generator. Building a wind turbine requires a few key components: blades, a rotor, a generator, and a tower. The blades, typically made from lightweight materials such as wood, fiberglass, or metal, capture the wind's energy and cause the rotor to spin. This spinning motion drives the generator, which produces electricity. The tower, which raises the turbine high above the ground, is crucial for accessing stronger and more consistent winds, as wind speeds generally increase with altitude.

Constructing a wind turbine from scratch can be challenging, especially without access to advanced tools and materials. However, repurposing materials from abandoned structures or scavenging parts from existing wind turbines can make the process more feasible. Maintenance is also a key consideration; regular inspections of the blades, bearings, and electrical connections are necessary to ensure the turbine operates efficiently. In regions where wind is a consistent and strong natural resource, wind turbines can provide a reliable source of electricity, particularly when combined with battery storage systems to capture energy for use during periods of calm.

In addition to wind power, water power offers another reliable energy source, particularly in areas with flowing rivers or streams. Water wheels and micro-hydro systems are effective ways to harness the energy of moving water. A water wheel, one of the oldest forms of mechanical energy conversion, uses the force of flowing water to turn a wheel, which can then power a mill, pump, or generator. Water wheels can be constructed from wood, metal, or a combination of both, depending on the resources available. The key to an effective water wheel is proper placement in a fast-moving section of a river or stream, where the flow of water can generate sufficient force to turn the wheel. This mechanical energy can be used directly for tasks such as grinding grain or can be converted into electricity with the addition of a generator.

Micro-hydro systems, on the other hand, are more sophisticated and are designed specifically for generating electricity. These systems divert a portion of a river or stream through a pipeline to a turbine, which spins a generator to produce electricity. Micro-hydro systems are particularly efficient because water, unlike wind or solar energy, provides a consistent and predictable power source, as long as the water flow is maintained. Constructing a micro-hydro system requires careful planning and understanding of the local water flow, as well as access to materials such as pipes, turbines, and generators. However, once established, these systems can provide a reliable and continuous supply of electricity with minimal maintenance.

Integrating wind and water energy into a community's energy grid involves more than just building the necessary infrastructure; it also requires coordination and management to ensure that the energy generated is used efficiently. Communities must establish protocols for distributing power, maintaining equipment, and balancing the load between different energy sources. For example, during periods of low wind, the community might rely more heavily on water or solar power, while during periods of drought, wind and solar might take precedence. Effective energy management ensures that all available resources are used to their fullest potential, reducing waste and maximizing the community's energy security.

In conclusion, wind and water power are invaluable resources for any community seeking to build a resilient and sustainable energy infrastructure. By mastering the construction and maintenance of wind turbines, water wheels, and micro-hydro systems, communities can diversify their energy sources and reduce their dependence on any single power source. This not only enhances the stability of their energy supply but also prepares them for a wide range of environmental conditions and challenges, ensuring that they can thrive even in the most difficult circumstances.

6.3 Bioenergy and Sustainable Fuels

In a post-collapse world, where traditional energy sources may become scarce or entirely unavailable, the ability to produce energy from organic materials is a crucial survival skill. Bioenergy, derived from biomass such as wood, agricultural waste, and organic matter, provides a renewable and sustainable source of fuel that can power homes, cook food, and even generate electricity. The key to leveraging bioenergy effectively lies in understanding how to convert raw organic materials into usable energy forms, such as biofuels, biogas, and charcoal. These methods not only reduce reliance on diminishing fossil fuel reserves but also help communities manage waste more sustainably by turning it into valuable resources.

One of the most practical applications of bioenergy is the production of biofuels, which can be created from a variety of organic materials, including crops, animal fats, and even algae. Biofuels, such as ethanol and biodiesel, can be produced through relatively simple processes that can be scaled according to the community's needs. For instance, ethanol can be made by fermenting sugar-rich crops like corn, sugarcane, or fruit waste. The fermentation process involves converting the sugars in these materials into alcohol using yeast, which can then be distilled to increase its purity. The resulting ethanol can be used as a fuel for modified engines, cooking stoves, or even as a disinfectant. Biodiesel, on the other hand, is produced by chemically reacting vegetable oils or animal fats with an alcohol like methanol in a process known as transesterification. The biodiesel produced can power diesel engines and generators, providing a sustainable alternative to traditional diesel fuel.

The production of biofuels requires not only the raw materials but also the appropriate equipment and knowledge. Distillation setups for ethanol can be constructed from basic materials like metal drums, copper tubing, and heat sources, while biodiesel production requires mixing tanks, separation units, and safety measures to handle the chemical reactions involved. Communities must also consider the sustainability of their feedstocks; using food crops for biofuel production might not be viable in a situation where food security is a concern. Therefore, focusing on non-food crops, agricultural waste, or even algae cultivation can provide a more sustainable feedstock for biofuel production. By mastering these processes, communities can create a local, renewable fuel supply that supports transportation, electricity generation, and cooking needs, reducing their dependence on external resources.

In addition to liquid biofuels, biogas is another valuable form of bioenergy that can be produced from organic waste materials. Biogas is primarily composed of methane and carbon dioxide, and it is generated through the anaerobic digestion of organic matter, such as animal manure, food waste, and plant material. This process occurs in a biogas digester, a sealed container where organic materials are broken down by bacteria in the absence of oxygen. The resulting biogas can be captured and used as a fuel for cooking, heating, or even generating electricity through a biogas generator. The digested material, known as digestate, is a nutrient-rich byproduct that can be used as a fertilizer, closing the loop in the community's waste management and agricultural processes.

Constructing a biogas digester can be done with locally available materials, such as large plastic or metal drums, pipes, and valves for gas collection. The digester must be airtight to ensure the anaerobic process, and it should be located in a warm area to maintain the activity of the bacteria. Regular feeding of the digester with organic waste and periodic stirring ensures efficient gas production. Communities can scale their biogas production to meet their energy needs, from small household digesters to larger community-scale systems. Biogas is especially valuable in areas where wood or other traditional fuels are scarce, providing a renewable and clean-burning alternative that can reduce deforestation and indoor air pollution.

Moreover, sustainable stoves and ovens designed to use biofuels or biogas can further enhance the efficiency of these energy sources. Traditional open fires, often used for cooking in resource-limited settings, are inefficient and produce harmful smoke that can lead to respiratory problems. In contrast, fuel-efficient stoves and ovens are designed to burn biofuels more completely, using less fuel and producing less smoke. Rocket stoves, for example, are highly efficient wood-burning stoves that use a small combustion chamber to create a hot, focused flame with minimal fuel. These stoves can be built using simple materials like bricks, metal cans, and insulation, making them accessible to communities with limited resources. Similarly, biogas stoves are designed to burn methane cleanly and efficiently, providing a safe and convenient way to cook food.

The integration of bioenergy into a community's energy mix not only provides a sustainable alternative to fossil fuels but also enhances resilience by utilizing local resources and reducing waste. By producing biofuels, biogas, and fuel-efficient stoves, communities can create a closed-loop system that supports their energy needs while promoting environmental sustainability. These technologies empower communities to become more self-sufficient, reducing their vulnerability to external energy disruptions and contributing to a more sustainable way of living.

6.4 Energy Storage Solutions

While generating renewable energy is essential for a self-sufficient community, the ability to store that energy for later use is equally important. Energy storage systems are crucial for managing the intermittent nature of renewable energy sources like solar and wind, which do not always produce power when it is needed. Effective energy storage solutions ensure that the energy generated during periods of abundance—such as sunny or windy days—can be saved and used during periods of scarcity, such as at night or on calm days. Understanding how to design, build, and maintain these storage systems is key to creating a reliable and resilient energy infrastructure.

Battery storage systems are among the most common and versatile methods for storing electrical energy. Batteries store energy in chemical form and release it as electricity when needed. There are several types of batteries that can be used for energy storage, including lead-acid, lithium-ion, and nickel-cadmium batteries, each with its advantages and drawbacks. Lead-acid batteries, for instance, are widely used in off-grid systems due to their reliability and relatively low cost, though they are heavy and have a limited lifespan. Lithium-ion batteries are more expensive but offer higher energy density, longer life, and greater efficiency. Nickel-cadmium batteries are durable and can operate in a wide range of temperatures but are less environmentally friendly due to the toxic materials they contain.

Designing a battery storage system involves determining the community's energy needs, selecting the appropriate type of battery, and configuring the system to store and deliver power efficiently. This includes sizing the battery bank to match the energy production and consumption patterns, ensuring proper ventilation to prevent overheating, and integrating charge controllers to protect the batteries from overcharging or deep discharge. It is also important to consider the safety aspects of battery storage, such as preventing short circuits, ensuring proper grounding, and regularly inspecting the batteries for signs of wear or damage.

Beyond electrical storage, thermal mass storage is another effective method for managing energy, particularly for heating and cooling applications. Thermal mass refers to materials that can absorb, store, and release heat energy over time. Common materials used for thermal mass storage include water, concrete, stone, and brick. These materials can be incorporated into building designs to regulate indoor temperatures, reducing the need for active heating and cooling systems. For example, a concrete floor or wall can absorb heat during the day and release it slowly at night, maintaining a more stable indoor temperature. This passive heating and cooling technique is especially valuable in climates with significant temperature fluctuations between day and night.

Thermal mass storage can also be used in conjunction with solar energy systems. For instance, solar water heaters can store thermal energy in water tanks, providing hot water even when the sun is not shining. Similarly, solar thermal panels can heat a thermal mass, such as a large masonry structure, which then radiates heat into a building during cooler periods. These systems are low-tech, require minimal maintenance, and can significantly reduce a community's reliance on conventional energy sources for heating and cooling.

Maintaining and repairing energy storage systems is crucial for ensuring their long-term reliability and efficiency. Batteries, for example, require regular maintenance, such as checking the electrolyte levels in lead-acid batteries, cleaning terminals, and equalizing charge levels to prevent sulfation. Lithium-ion batteries, while lower maintenance, need to be monitored for overheating and voltage imbalances. For thermal mass systems, maintenance might involve inspecting insulation, sealing cracks in masonry, or ensuring that heat transfer systems are functioning properly. Communities should train members in the basics of energy storage maintenance and repair, empowering them to troubleshoot issues and extend the lifespan of these critical systems.

Furthermore, the integration of energy storage systems into the broader community energy grid requires careful planning and management. Balancing the load between generation, storage, and consumption is essential to avoid overloading systems or running out of stored energy during critical times. Smart inverters and energy management systems can help automate this process, ensuring that energy is used efficiently and that storage systems are charged and discharged at optimal times. In a resource-constrained environment, such management is crucial for maximizing the utility of every watt of power generated and stored.

In conclusion, energy storage solutions are a cornerstone of a resilient and sustainable energy infrastructure. By mastering the design, construction, and maintenance of battery storage systems, thermal mass storage, and other energy storage technologies, communities can ensure a stable and reliable energy supply, even when renewable energy sources are intermittent. These systems not only enhance the efficiency and reliability of the community's energy grid but also provide a critical buffer against energy shortages, ensuring that the community can thrive even in the most challenging conditions.

6.5 Energy Conservation Strategies

While generating and storing energy is crucial for any self-sufficient community, equally important is the efficient use of that energy. Energy conservation strategies are essential for minimizing waste, reducing the overall demand on energy systems, and ensuring that available resources are used as effectively as possible. By focusing on energy conservation, communities can stretch their energy supplies further, reduce the frequency of power shortages, and enhance their overall sustainability. These strategies not only help in managing scarce resources but also contribute to a more comfortable and resilient living environment.

One of the most effective ways to conserve energy is through proper insulation of homes and communal buildings. Insulation plays a critical role in maintaining indoor temperatures, reducing the need for heating in the winter and cooling in the summer. Well-insulated buildings retain heat during cold periods and keep the interior cool during hot weather, thus reducing the reliance on active heating and cooling systems, which are often energy-intensive. There are various materials that can be used for insulation, depending on availability and the specific needs of the building. Common insulation materials include fiberglass, cellulose, foam, and natural materials like straw, wool, or recycled textiles. In a post-collapse scenario, communities may need to get creative with insulation materials, using whatever is readily available, such as old clothing, newspapers, or even earth.

The key areas to insulate include walls, roofs, floors, and windows. Double-glazing windows or using heavy curtains can significantly reduce heat loss, while insulating the attic or roof space prevents warm air from escaping upwards. Draft-proofing doors and windows is another simple yet effective measure; even small gaps can lead to significant energy loss. Sealing these gaps with weatherstripping or caulking ensures that the warm air stays inside during winter and that cool air is preserved during summer. In addition to these measures, designing buildings with energy efficiency in mind, such as incorporating passive solar design, can also reduce the energy needed to maintain comfortable temperatures. For example, placing windows on the south side of a building in the Northern Hemisphere maximizes solar gain in the winter, while overhangs or shading devices can reduce heat during the summer.

Beyond structural improvements, energy-efficient cooking and heating systems are critical for conserving energy in daily life. Traditional open fires and inefficient stoves consume large amounts of fuel, much of which is wasted in the form of heat loss. By contrast, fuel-efficient stoves, such as rocket stoves, are designed to burn fuel more completely and direct more of the heat to the cooking surface or into the living space. Rocket stoves achieve this by using an insulated combustion chamber that ensures a hotter and more efficient burn, requiring less fuel to achieve the same cooking or heating results. These stoves can be constructed from simple materials like bricks, metal cans, or clay, making them accessible even in resource-scarce environments. Similarly, solar cookers and ovens, which use reflective surfaces to concentrate sunlight for cooking, provide an energy-free alternative to traditional cooking methods, particularly in sunny climates.

For heating, the use of thermal mass and efficient wood stoves can significantly reduce the amount of fuel needed. Thermal mass, as discussed earlier, involves using materials that absorb and slowly release heat, such as stone, concrete, or water. Incorporating thermal mass into a building's design helps maintain a stable indoor temperature, reducing the need for additional heating. For example, a masonry heater, which is a type of wood stove built with a large thermal mass, can store heat from a single, efficient fire and radiate it for hours, providing consistent warmth with minimal fuel use. These systems are particularly effective in cold climates, where the need for heating is constant and fuel resources may be limited.

Another critical aspect of energy conservation is community energy management and rationing. In a post-collapse environment, energy resources are likely to be limited, making it necessary to prioritize their use. Establishing a system of energy rationing ensures that all members of the community have access to the energy they need while preventing overuse and waste. This might involve setting limits on the amount of electricity or fuel each household can use, scheduling times for communal cooking or heating, or rotating the use of high-energy appliances like generators or pumps. Rationing can be managed through simple systems like token distribution, where each household receives a certain number of energy tokens that can be exchanged for fuel, electricity, or access to communal energy resources.

Community energy management also involves educating members about energy conservation practices and encouraging behavioral changes that reduce energy consumption. This can include turning off lights and appliances when not in use, using energy-efficient cooking methods, sharing rides to reduce fuel consumption, and optimizing the use of natural light and ventilation to reduce the need for artificial lighting and cooling. Regular community meetings can be used to discuss energy usage, share tips and techniques for conserving energy, and address any issues or concerns related to energy rationing. By fostering a culture of energy awareness and cooperation, communities can ensure that their energy resources are used wisely and sustainably.

Finally, it is important to consider the long-term sustainability of energy conservation strategies. As communities grow and evolve, their energy needs will change, and so too must their conservation strategies. Continuous monitoring of energy usage, regular maintenance of energy systems, and ongoing education about energy conservation are all necessary to maintain efficiency and adapt to new challenges. By making energy conservation a core part of their survival strategy, communities can build a resilient and sustainable energy infrastructure that supports their long-term survival and prosperity.

In conclusion, energy conservation strategies are essential for any community striving for self-sufficiency and sustainability. By insulating buildings, using energy-efficient cooking and heating systems, and implementing community-wide energy management practices, communities can significantly reduce their energy consumption and extend the life of their energy resources. These strategies not only make the most of the energy that is available but also help create a more resilient and sustainable living environment, ensuring that the community can thrive even in the face of limited resources and challenging conditions.

Chapter 7: Rebuilding Governance and Social Structures

Strong leadership and fair governance are vital for social cohesion. This chapter discusses how to establish effective leadership, create laws, and build a culture that supports cooperation, justice, and community resilience.

7.1 Establishing Leadership

In the aftermath of a societal collapse, the establishment of effective leadership is one of the most critical steps toward rebuilding a functional and resilient community. Without strong and reliable leadership, efforts to organize, protect, and sustain the group can quickly unravel into chaos and discord. Leadership in this context is not about exerting power for its own sake but about guiding the community through difficult decisions, coordinating resources, and fostering a sense of unity and purpose. To achieve this, it is essential to identify natural leaders within the community, create a governance structure that promotes participation, and establish decision-making processes that are transparent and inclusive.

Identifying natural leaders in a community involves recognizing individuals who possess the qualities necessary to inspire trust and cooperation among their peers. These qualities include integrity, empathy, problem-solving skills, and the ability to remain calm and focused under pressure. Natural leaders often emerge organically in times of crisis—those who are willing to take responsibility, offer solutions, and bring people together are likely candidates for leadership roles. However, it is important that leadership is not concentrated in the hands of a single individual; instead, a leadership team or council should be formed to distribute responsibilities and ensure that a range of perspectives is considered in decision-making.

Creating a council or governance body is a key step in formalizing leadership within the community. This council should consist of individuals who represent different segments of the community, ensuring that the diverse needs and concerns of the population are addressed. For example, the council might include leaders from various family groups, skilled tradespeople, healthcare providers, and those responsible for security and resource management. The council's primary role is to make decisions that benefit the entire community, allocate resources, and resolve conflicts. To function effectively, the council must operate with transparency, regularly communicating its decisions and the rationale behind them to the rest of the community.

Decision-making processes within the council should be designed to encourage participation from all members of the community, not just the council members themselves. This can be achieved through regular meetings where community members are invited to voice their opinions, propose solutions, and vote on key issues. Participatory decision-making fosters a sense of ownership and responsibility among community members, which is crucial for maintaining social cohesion and trust. In addition, it ensures that decisions are made with the input of those who will be most affected by them, leading to more sustainable and widely supported outcomes.

To avoid the pitfalls of centralized power, the council should also establish mechanisms for accountability. This includes setting term limits for council members, allowing for regular elections or rotations in leadership positions, and creating a system for removing or replacing leaders who are not fulfilling their duties. By ensuring that leadership remains dynamic and responsive to the community's needs, these mechanisms help prevent the abuse of power and maintain the legitimacy of the governance structure.

In summary, establishing leadership in a post-collapse community involves identifying natural leaders, creating a governance council that represents the entire community, and developing decision-making processes that are inclusive and transparent. By fostering a leadership structure that encourages participation and accountability, the community can build a strong foundation for effective governance and long-term resilience.

7.2 Creating Laws and Regulations

Once a leadership structure is in place, the next critical step in rebuilding governance is the establishment of laws and regulations that provide a framework for maintaining order, ensuring fairness, and promoting the well-being of the community. In a world where established legal systems may no longer function, communities must create their own code of conduct tailored to their unique circumstances and values. This process involves not only drafting and enforcing rules but also adapting them as the community evolves and grows. Additionally, setting up mechanisms for conflict resolution, addressing grievances, and rehabilitating offenders is essential for maintaining peace and justice within the community.

The first task in creating laws and regulations is to establish a code of conduct that outlines the basic principles and rules that all community members are expected to follow. This code should reflect the core values of the community, such as respect for others, cooperation, honesty, and the protection of shared resources. The process of drafting this code should be collaborative, with input from a wide range of community members to ensure that the rules are fair, relevant, and widely accepted. The code of conduct should address key areas such as property rights, resource allocation, interpersonal behavior, and the consequences for violating the rules.

Once the code of conduct is established, the community must develop a system for enforcing these rules fairly and consistently. This requires the establishment of a group or individual responsible for monitoring compliance and addressing violations. In many cases, this role may be fulfilled by a designated council member or a small team tasked with upholding the community's laws. It is crucial that enforcement is carried out impartially, without favoritism or bias, to maintain the integrity of the legal system and the trust of the community.

As the community grows and evolves, it will be necessary to adapt and expand the laws to address new challenges and circumstances. This may include creating more detailed regulations around resource management, trade, and interactions with other communities. The process of adapting laws should be flexible and responsive to the changing needs of the community, with regular reviews and opportunities for community members to propose changes or new regulations. By keeping the legal framework dynamic, the community can ensure that its laws remain relevant and effective.

In addition to establishing rules and enforcing them, it is important to set up a system for resolving disputes and addressing grievances within the community. This can be achieved by creating a community court or mediation system where conflicts can be aired and resolved in a fair and transparent manner. The court or mediation body should be composed of respected community members who are seen as impartial and capable of making balanced judgments. Their role is to listen to both sides of a dispute, consider the evidence, and provide a resolution that is in line with the community's laws and values. By providing a structured process for conflict resolution, the community can prevent disputes from escalating into violence or division.

Addressing grievances is not just about resolving disputes but also about maintaining social harmony and ensuring that all community members feel heard and respected. This includes providing avenues for individuals to express their concerns and frustrations, whether through formal channels like the community court or more informal settings like community meetings. By addressing grievances promptly and fairly, the community can prevent small issues from growing into larger problems that could threaten the social fabric.

Finally, a critical aspect of maintaining peace and justice within the community is the rehabilitation and reintegration of offenders. In a small, close-knit community, the goal should not only be to punish wrongdoers but also to help them reintegrate into the community as productive members. This might involve restorative justice practices, where offenders are required to make amends to those they have harmed, as well as providing opportunities for education, skill-building, or other forms of support that can help them avoid future offenses. By focusing on rehabilitation rather than retribution, the community can strengthen social bonds and reduce the likelihood of recurring conflicts.

In conclusion, creating laws and regulations in a post-collapse community involves establishing a code of conduct, enforcing rules fairly, adapting laws as needed, and setting up systems for conflict resolution and rehabilitation. These legal frameworks are essential for maintaining order, ensuring fairness, and fostering a sense of justice and community cohesion. By building a legal system that is flexible, fair, and focused on the well-being of all members, the community can create a stable and just society that is capable of withstanding the challenges of a post-collapse world.

7.3 Building a Resilient Culture

Building a resilient culture is the cornerstone of any successful community, particularly in a post-collapse world where traditional societal structures have broken down. Culture serves as the glue that binds a community together, offering a shared identity, values, and sense of purpose that guide collective actions. In the absence of the old societal norms, the task of creating a new culture becomes not just important but essential for the survival and thriving of the group. This culture must be rooted in principles that promote cooperation, adaptability, and sustainability, while also honoring and preserving the unique achievements and traditions that emerge within the community.

One of the first steps in cultivating a resilient culture is to actively celebrate the community's achievements and milestones. In a world where the daily struggle for survival can easily overshadow moments of progress, it is crucial to create space for recognition and celebration. These moments of acknowledgment help reinforce the community's collective spirit, providing psychological and emotional sustenance that can fortify the group against the hardships they face. Whether it is the successful completion of a harvest, the construction of a new shelter, or the birth of a child, celebrating these events reinforces the community's shared goals and the value of every member's contributions. These celebrations also serve to cement memories that can be passed down through stories and rituals, becoming a part of the community's evolving narrative.

Traditions play a pivotal role in the formation and preservation of culture. In the wake of a collapse, some pre-existing traditions may no longer be relevant or feasible, while new ones will need to be created to suit the community's current reality. The creation of new traditions should be an organic process, one that arises naturally from the community's experiences, values, and needs. For example, the community might establish a yearly festival to mark the start of the growing season, or a communal meal to celebrate the end of the harvest. These traditions, while simple, help to instill a sense of normalcy and continuity, offering a rhythm to life that contrasts with the uncertainties of the outside world. Over time, these traditions become part of the community's identity, providing comfort and a sense of belonging to its members.

A resilient culture must also promote the values of cooperation and mutual aid. In a survival scenario, individualism can be detrimental to the well-being of the group. Instead, the culture should emphasize the importance of working together, sharing resources, and supporting one another. This can be encouraged through community activities that require collective effort, such as building projects, communal gardening, or group hunting expeditions. These activities not only provide essential resources but also foster strong interpersonal bonds and a sense of collective responsibility. By embedding the value of cooperation into the daily life of the community, these practices become second nature, reducing conflicts and ensuring that the group can operate as a cohesive unit in the face of challenges.

Sustainability is another core principle that must be integrated into the community's culture. In a post-collapse world, the careless exploitation of resources can lead to disaster. A sustainable culture recognizes the finite nature of these resources and prioritizes their careful management and renewal. This involves teaching community members to live within their means, minimize waste, and use resources in a way that preserves them for future generations. For example, agricultural practices should emphasize crop rotation, composting, and the use of natural fertilizers to maintain soil health. Similarly, the community should prioritize the use of renewable energy sources, such as solar or wind power, and develop technologies that minimize environmental impact. By making sustainability a cultural norm, the community ensures its long-term viability and reduces its vulnerability to external shocks.

Art, music, and literature play a critical role in reflecting and shaping the community's culture. In the absence of formal institutions, these creative expressions become the primary means of preserving the community's experiences, values, and aspirations. Encouraging the creation of art that reflects the community's struggles and triumphs not only provides a therapeutic outlet for individuals but also helps to build a collective identity. Songs that tell the stories of the community's history, paintings that depict significant events, and literature that explores the community's values all contribute to a rich cultural tapestry. These creative works can be passed down through generations, ensuring that the community's cultural heritage is preserved even as it continues to evolve.

Moreover, a resilient culture must be flexible and adaptable, capable of evolving in response to changing circumstances. This adaptability is crucial in a post-collapse environment, where the challenges and threats faced by the community can shift rapidly. A rigid culture that cannot accommodate change risks becoming obsolete or even harmful. Instead, the community should cultivate a culture that values innovation, experimentation, and learning. This might involve regular community discussions about what is working and what is not, encouraging members to propose new ideas and solutions, and being willing to adjust or abandon practices that no longer serve the community's best interests. By fostering a culture of continuous learning and adaptation, the community not only survives but thrives in an unpredictable world.

In conclusion, building a resilient culture is about more than just preserving traditions or celebrating achievements—it is about creating a living, breathing framework that supports the community's survival and growth. By emphasizing cooperation, sustainability, and adaptability, and by encouraging creative expression, the community can forge a strong cultural identity that unites its members and prepares them to face the future together. This culture will serve as the foundation upon which all other aspects of the community—its governance, economy, and social structures—are built, ensuring that the group remains resilient and cohesive in the face of whatever challenges lie ahead.

Chapter 8: Health and Medicine in a New World

Health is the foundation of a thriving community. This chapter covers how to build a community health system, integrate traditional and modern medicine, and prepare for medical emergencies in a world where resources are limited.

8.1 Building a Community Health System

In a post-collapse world, where modern healthcare infrastructure may be severely compromised or entirely absent, the establishment of a robust community health system becomes a critical priority. Without access to the vast resources of hospitals, pharmacies, and trained medical personnel, communities must take responsibility for their own health needs. This involves identifying and training healthcare providers from within the community, setting up a basic health facility, and ensuring a steady supply of essential medical resources. By building a community health system from the ground up, communities can significantly improve their resilience, reduce mortality rates, and enhance the overall quality of life for their members.

The first step in establishing a community health system is identifying individuals within the community who possess or can acquire the skills necessary to provide healthcare. These individuals may already have some medical training, such as former nurses, paramedics, or doctors, but it's equally important to identify those who are willing and able to learn. Training programs should be implemented to teach basic medical skills, such as wound care, the administration of first aid, and the recognition of common illnesses. These programs can be facilitated by the more experienced healthcare providers in the community or through the use of instructional manuals and resources that can be scavenged or created. The goal is to develop a cadre of community health workers who can provide care, offer guidance on health matters, and educate others on preventive practices.

Once healthcare providers are identified and trained, the next step is to establish a community clinic or health post. This facility does not need to be elaborate, but it should be equipped to handle basic medical needs such as treating minor injuries, managing chronic conditions, and addressing common illnesses. The clinic should be centrally located to ensure accessibility for all community members and should include spaces for patient consultation, treatment, and storage of medical supplies. Basic equipment such as examination tables, sterilization tools, and medical instruments should be prioritized, along with the creation of a clean and sanitary environment to reduce the risk of infection. If possible, the clinic should also include a dedicated area for quarantine in case of infectious disease outbreaks.

A crucial aspect of the community health system is establishing a reliable medical supply chain. Without the ability to easily purchase or produce medical supplies, communities must develop innovative ways to obtain, store, and distribute essential items such as bandages, antiseptics, medications, and surgical tools. This might involve scavenging abandoned pharmacies and medical facilities, trading with neighboring communities, or even learning to manufacture certain supplies locally. For example, simple bandages can be made from clean cloth, while basic antiseptics can be produced from alcohol or iodine. Establishing a central storage area for these supplies, with careful inventory management, ensures that the community can respond effectively to medical needs as they arise. The supply chain should also include a plan for securing and storing critical medications, particularly those with a long shelf life or that are difficult to obtain.

In addition to physical supplies, a sustainable community health system must also focus on knowledge and education. This includes training healthcare providers in both modern and traditional medical practices, as well as educating the broader community about health and hygiene. Regular workshops, informational sessions, and training exercises can help disseminate critical health information and ensure that all community members are equipped to maintain their health and prevent the spread of disease. By building a culture of health consciousness, the community can reduce the burden on the healthcare system and improve overall well-being.

8.2 Traditional and Herbal Medicine

In a world where access to modern medicine may be limited or nonexistent, traditional and herbal medicine becomes an invaluable resource for maintaining health and treating illness. Long before the advent of pharmaceuticals, people relied on the healing properties of plants and other natural substances to treat a wide range of ailments. Reviving this knowledge and integrating it with modern medical practices can provide communities with a powerful toolset for addressing health challenges in a post-collapse environment. By identifying and using medicinal plants, preparing and storing herbal remedies, and blending traditional practices with modern medicine, communities can enhance their self-reliance and improve their ability to care for the sick and injured.

The first step in harnessing the power of traditional and herbal medicine is to identify the medicinal plants that grow in the local environment. This requires a deep understanding of the local flora, as well as knowledge of which plants have therapeutic properties. In many regions, this knowledge may still exist within older generations or among those who practiced herbal medicine before the collapse. These individuals can be invaluable resources for teaching others about plant identification, harvesting techniques, and the preparation of remedies. Communities should make efforts to document this knowledge, creating written records or instructional guides that can be passed down and preserved for future generations.

Once the appropriate plants have been identified, the next step is to learn how to properly prepare and store herbal remedies. Different plants require different methods of preparation to unlock their medicinal properties. Some may need to be dried and ground into powders, while others are best used fresh in teas, poultices, or tinctures. It is important to learn these techniques to ensure that the remedies are both effective and safe. Drying herbs is one of the most common methods of preservation, as it allows the plant material to be stored for long periods without losing its potency. Herbs can be dried by hanging them in a well-ventilated area out of direct sunlight or by using solar dehydrators. Once dried, the herbs should be stored in airtight containers in a cool, dark place to maintain their effectiveness.

Tinctures, which are concentrated liquid extracts made by soaking herbs in alcohol or vinegar, are another popular form of herbal remedy. These can be particularly useful because they have a long shelf life and are easy to administer. Learning to make tinctures involves understanding the correct ratios of plant material to solvent and the appropriate soaking times to extract the active compounds. Similarly, salves and ointments can be made by infusing herbs into oils or fats, which can then be applied topically to treat wounds, rashes, and other skin conditions. By mastering these preparation techniques, communities can create a versatile herbal medicine cabinet capable of addressing a wide range of health issues.

Integrating traditional practices with modern medicine is another key aspect of creating a holistic community health system. While modern medicine excels in areas such as emergency care and surgery, traditional medicine offers valuable approaches to chronic conditions, preventive care, and overall wellness. For example, while antibiotics might be used to treat a severe infection, herbal remedies could be employed to support the immune system and aid in recovery. In cases where modern medications are unavailable, traditional remedies may provide an effective alternative. However, it is crucial to approach this integration with a careful, evidence-based mindset. Not all traditional practices are beneficial, and some may be harmful if used improperly. Therefore, communities should prioritize ongoing education and research, drawing from both scientific and traditional knowledge to determine the most effective treatments.

Moreover, the use of traditional and herbal medicine fosters a sense of connection to the natural world, which can be particularly important in a post-collapse environment. This connection reinforces the idea that the community is part of a larger ecosystem and that by caring for the environment, they are also caring for their own health. Encouraging sustainable harvesting practices, protecting local habitats, and cultivating medicinal plants in community gardens are all ways to ensure that these resources remain available for future generations. By embedding traditional and herbal medicine into the fabric of the community's health system, the group not only gains practical tools for survival but also strengthens its cultural and environmental ties.

In summary, traditional and herbal medicine offers a valuable complement to modern healthcare practices, particularly in a world where access to conventional medicine is limited. By identifying medicinal plants, mastering preparation and storage techniques, and integrating these practices with modern medicine, communities can build a more resilient and self-sufficient health system. This approach not only enhances the community's ability to care for its members but also fosters a deeper connection to the natural world and the cultural traditions that sustain it.

8.3 Preventive Healthcare and Hygiene

In a post-collapse world, where medical resources are scarce and professional healthcare may be limited, preventive healthcare and hygiene become the front lines in the battle against disease and illness. Without the luxury of modern medical infrastructure, the emphasis must shift from treating illnesses after they occur to preventing them from happening in the first place. This proactive approach is not only more sustainable but also crucial for the survival of the community. By understanding the importance of cleanliness, adopting effective sanitation practices, and promoting a culture of health, communities can significantly reduce the burden of disease and improve the overall quality of life.

The foundation of preventive healthcare in any community is cleanliness and sanitation. Clean living environments are essential to prevent the spread of infectious diseases, which can quickly decimate populations that lack access to adequate medical care. Proper waste management, regular cleaning of communal areas, and the maintenance of personal hygiene are critical components of this strategy. Communities must establish and enforce standards for waste disposal, ensuring that garbage is collected and processed in a way that does not attract pests or contaminate water sources. Composting toilets, greywater systems, and the careful management of organic waste can all contribute to maintaining a sanitary environment. Regular cleaning of living spaces, particularly areas where food is prepared and consumed, is also vital to prevent the buildup of harmful bacteria and other pathogens.

Hand hygiene is perhaps the most basic yet effective method for preventing the spread of disease. In the absence of modern plumbing, communities must find alternative ways to ensure that clean water and soap are available for handwashing. This might involve setting up communal handwashing stations equipped with simple foot-pump-operated water dispensers and soap. Educating community members, particularly children, about the importance of regular handwashing—especially after using the toilet, before eating, and after handling waste—is crucial. Additionally, making hand sanitizer using alcohol-based solutions can provide a backup when water is scarce. By ingraining these practices into daily routines, the community can create a culture of cleanliness that serves as a first line of defense against disease.

Sanitation practices extend beyond personal hygiene to include the safe preparation and storage of food and water. Contaminated food and water are common vectors for disease, and in a survival scenario, the community cannot afford widespread illness caused by preventable contamination. Proper cooking techniques, such as boiling water and thoroughly cooking meat, are essential for killing harmful pathogens. Food should be stored in secure, clean containers to prevent exposure to pests and bacteria. Additionally, communities should prioritize the construction of safe water collection and storage systems, such as rainwater harvesting setups with filtration systems, to ensure a reliable supply of clean drinking water.

Regular inspection and maintenance of these systems are necessary to prevent contamination and ensure their continued effectiveness.

Vaccination, where possible, remains one of the most effective tools for preventing the spread of infectious diseases. While access to vaccines may be limited in a post-collapse world, any available vaccines should be prioritized and distributed to those most at risk, such as children, the elderly, and those with compromised immune systems. Communities should make efforts to acquire and store vaccines, possibly through barter or trade with other groups, and maintain cold storage facilities to preserve them. Education about the importance of vaccination and the diseases they prevent can help reduce hesitancy and ensure high uptake among community members. Where modern vaccines are unavailable, alternative strategies such as isolation of infected individuals, quarantine measures, and the promotion of herd immunity through natural exposure might need to be employed, though these come with significant risks.

Promoting healthy lifestyles and nutrition is another cornerstone of preventive healthcare. Proper nutrition is essential for maintaining a strong immune system, which in turn helps to fend off infections and diseases. In a post-collapse environment, where food sources may be limited, communities must focus on cultivating a balanced diet through sustainable agriculture. This includes growing a variety of crops that provide essential vitamins and minerals, raising livestock for protein, and foraging for wild edibles that can supplement the diet. Educating community members about the importance of a balanced diet and the nutritional value of locally available foods is key to ensuring that everyone has access to the nutrients they need to stay healthy.

Physical activity is also important for maintaining overall health. While daily survival tasks such as farming, hunting, and building provide some level of physical exertion, it is important to encourage additional forms of exercise that promote cardiovascular health, flexibility, and strength. Community activities, such as group walks, sports, or dance, can not only improve physical health but also strengthen social bonds and boost morale. Ensuring that all members of the community, regardless of age or physical ability, have opportunities to stay active contributes to a healthier, more resilient population.

Mental health is another critical aspect of preventive healthcare. The stresses of living in a post-collapse world, combined with the loss of loved ones and the daily struggle for survival, can take a significant toll on mental well-being. Communities must recognize the importance of mental health and provide support systems to help individuals cope with stress, anxiety, and trauma. This might involve setting up peer support groups, providing spaces for relaxation and reflection, and encouraging open communication about mental health issues. Activities that promote mental wellness, such as meditation, storytelling, and communal gatherings, can help build resilience and ensure that the community remains strong in the face of adversity.

In summary, preventive healthcare and hygiene are the bedrock of a resilient community in a post-collapse world. By prioritizing cleanliness, sanitation, vaccination, and healthy lifestyles, communities can prevent the spread of disease and maintain a high standard of health despite limited resources. These practices, when integrated into the daily life of the community, create a culture of health that not only enhances individual well-being but also strengthens the collective resilience of the group, ensuring its survival and prosperity in the long term.

8.4 Emergency Medical Response

In a world where access to professional medical care is limited or nonexistent, the ability to respond effectively to medical emergencies becomes a critical component of community survival. Whether dealing with injuries, sudden illnesses, or large-scale disease outbreaks, a well-prepared emergency medical response system can save lives and prevent minor issues from escalating into major crises. Establishing such a system requires training community members in essential medical skills, creating a network of first responders, and developing clear protocols for handling various types of medical emergencies. By building a robust emergency medical response infrastructure, communities can ensure that they are equipped to handle the inevitable health challenges that will arise in a post-collapse environment.

The foundation of any emergency medical response system is the training of individuals who can act as first responders. These first responders are the community's frontline defense against medical emergencies, capable of providing immediate care in the crucial minutes or hours before more advanced treatment can be administered. Training programs should focus on teaching basic first aid, CPR, wound management, and the stabilization of injuries such as fractures and sprains. These skills can be taught by more experienced healthcare providers within the community or through the use of manuals and instructional materials. It is important that training is not limited to a select few but is made accessible to as many community members as possible, ensuring that there is always someone nearby who can respond in an emergency.

Once a core group of first responders is trained, the next step is to organize them into a network that can be mobilized quickly when needed. This network should include individuals from various parts of the community, ensuring broad coverage and the ability to respond rapidly to emergencies wherever they occur. Communication systems, such as hand-held radios or signal systems, should be established to alert first responders to an emergency and coordinate their actions. It is also important to conduct regular drills and simulations to ensure that the response network is well-practiced and able to function effectively under pressure. These drills should cover a range of scenarios, from individual injuries to larger-scale incidents like fires, natural disasters, or disease outbreaks, allowing first responders to build the experience and confidence needed to act swiftly and decisively.

Developing protocols for handling different types of medical emergencies is another critical aspect of emergency medical response. These protocols provide a clear, step-by-step guide for first responders and other community members to follow, ensuring that everyone knows what to do in an emergency and that actions are coordinated and efficient. Protocols should cover the full spectrum of potential emergencies, from minor injuries to life-threatening situations. For example, a protocol for a serious injury might include steps such as assessing the scene for safety, controlling bleeding, immobilizing the injury, and preparing the patient for transport to a medical facility. In the case of a disease outbreak, protocols might include identifying and isolating the infected individuals, implementing quarantine measures, and providing supportive care while monitoring the spread of the disease.

In addition to physical injuries, communities must also be prepared to respond to psychological emergencies, which can arise in the aftermath of traumatic events. The mental health of community members is as important as their physical health, and protocols should include steps for providing emotional support, identifying individuals who may be at risk for mental health issues, and connecting them with appropriate resources or counseling. First responders should be trained to recognize the signs of psychological distress and to approach these situations with empathy and care, helping to prevent the long-term psychological impact of trauma.

Creating and maintaining emergency medical supplies is another vital component of the response system. A well-stocked first aid kit should be available in key locations throughout the community, such as at the health clinic, communal gathering areas, and in the homes of trained first responders. These kits should include essentials such as bandages, antiseptics, pain relievers, splints, and emergency blankets, as well as any specialized items needed for specific conditions or common injuries in the area. Communities should also establish a system for regularly checking and replenishing these supplies to ensure that they are always ready for use.

Moreover, transportation is a critical aspect of emergency medical response, particularly in situations where advanced care is needed beyond what first responders can provide. In a post-collapse world, where motorized vehicles may be scarce or unreliable, communities must develop alternative methods for transporting patients to medical facilities or other safe locations. This might include the use of carts, stretchers, or even makeshift litters that can be carried by multiple people. The community should also plan for the construction of safe and accessible routes to and from key locations, ensuring that patients can be transported quickly and safely in an emergency.

In conclusion, building an effective emergency medical response system is essential for the survival of a community in a post-collapse world. By training first responders, organizing a response network, developing emergency protocols, and ensuring the availability of medical supplies and transportation, communities can be better prepared to handle medical emergencies and reduce the impact of health crises. This preparedness not only saves lives but also enhances the overall resilience of the community, ensuring that it can weather the challenges of a world where professional medical care is no longer readily available.

Chapter 9: Education and Knowledge Preservation

Knowledge is power, and education is key to rebuilding civilization. This chapter emphasizes the importance of preserving and transmitting knowledge through practical skills, science, and technology to future-proof your community.

9.1 Establishing a Learning Environment

In the aftermath of a societal collapse, the importance of education cannot be overstated. As communities begin the arduous task of rebuilding, the preservation and transmission of knowledge become crucial to ensuring that the hard-won lessons of the past are not lost and that future generations are equipped with the skills needed to thrive. Establishing a learning environment is the first step toward reviving education in a world where traditional schools and educational institutions may no longer exist. This task involves creating makeshift classrooms, recruiting educators and knowledgeable community members, and designing a curriculum that prioritizes survival, rebuilding, and the long-term prosperity of the community.

Creating makeshift classrooms is a practical solution to the absence of formal educational spaces. These classrooms do not need to be elaborate; they can be set up in any available shelter, such as a community center, a large room in a communal building, or even outdoors under a sturdy canopy. The key is to create a dedicated space where learning can take place consistently and without interruption. This space should be arranged to foster focus and engagement, with seating arranged in a way that facilitates interaction and group work. If possible, basic supplies such as chalkboards, writing materials, and books should be gathered and made available to students. In the absence of these materials, creative alternatives can be employed—such as using flat stones or wooden boards as slates, and charcoal or sharpened sticks for writing.

Recruiting educators and knowledgeable community members is a crucial step in establishing a learning environment. In a post-collapse scenario, the traditional roles of teachers may need to be redefined. Educators could be anyone in the community who possesses valuable knowledge or skills, whether or not they have formal teaching experience. These individuals might include former teachers, tradespeople, farmers, or elders with deep knowledge of traditional practices. The goal is to draw on the collective wisdom of the community to educate the younger generation and pass on the skills necessary for survival and rebuilding. These educators should be encouraged to share not only their expertise but also their passion for learning and innovation, fostering a culture of curiosity and resilience within the community.

Designing a curriculum focused on survival and rebuilding is essential for ensuring that education remains relevant to the community's immediate needs. This curriculum should go beyond traditional academic subjects to include practical, hands-on skills that are crucial for day-to-day survival in a world where modern conveniences are no longer available. Subjects such as basic literacy and numeracy remain important, but they should be integrated with lessons on topics like farming, food preservation, construction, and basic healthcare. The curriculum should also include lessons on leadership, ethics, and community building, to prepare students not only to survive but to take active roles in the governance and development of their community. Flexibility is key, as the curriculum may need to evolve over time to address new challenges and opportunities as they arise.

To foster a well-rounded education, it is important to balance these practical lessons with opportunities for creative and critical thinking. This might involve incorporating storytelling, arts, and music into the curriculum, which can help preserve the cultural heritage of the community while also allowing students to express themselves and explore new ideas. Encouraging students to ask questions, explore their environment, and come up with innovative solutions to problems will help them develop the critical thinking and problem-solving skills that are vital in a rapidly changing world. By establishing a learning environment that values both practical skills and intellectual curiosity, the community can equip its members with the knowledge and mindset needed to rebuild and thrive in the long term.

9.2 Teaching Practical Skills

In a world where the conveniences of modern life have disappeared, teaching practical skills becomes a cornerstone of education. These skills are not just useful—they are essential for survival and the successful rebuilding of the community. Prioritizing the teaching of essential survival skills, incorporating hands-on learning, and encouraging problem-solving and innovation are critical steps in creating a resilient and self-sufficient population. The focus of education must shift from abstract knowledge to practical application, ensuring that every member of the community, regardless of age, is equipped to contribute to the collective effort of survival and reconstruction.

The first priority in this new educational paradigm is to teach essential survival skills. These include farming, foraging, hunting, and fishing, which are necessary for food security. Understanding how to cultivate crops, raise livestock, and preserve food through methods such as drying, salting, and canning will ensure that the community can sustain itself even in the face of adversity. Construction skills, such as building shelters, making tools, and maintaining infrastructure, are also crucial. These skills not only provide the physical means to rebuild but also empower individuals with the knowledge to repair and innovate as needed. Additionally, basic healthcare skills—such as first aid, wound care, and the use of herbal remedies—are vital in a context where access to modern medicine may be limited. These skills ensure that minor injuries and illnesses do not escalate into life-threatening conditions.

Incorporating hands-on learning is key to effectively teaching these practical skills. Unlike traditional classroom settings where students might learn from textbooks and lectures, the new educational approach must emphasize learning by doing. For example, rather than merely teaching students about farming techniques in theory, they should be taken to the fields to plant, tend, and harvest crops themselves. Similarly, lessons on construction should involve actual building projects, such as constructing a new shelter or repairing community infrastructure. This approach not only reinforces the knowledge being taught but also allows students to develop the muscle memory and confidence needed to perform these tasks independently. Hands-on learning also fosters a deeper connection between the students and their environment, helping them to understand the practical implications of their actions and decisions.

Encouraging problem-solving and innovation is another critical component of teaching practical skills. In a world where resources are limited and challenges are constant, the ability to think creatively and adapt to new situations is invaluable. Educators should create opportunities for students to tackle real-world problems, whether it's finding a way to improve crop yields, designing more efficient tools, or developing new methods for water purification. These challenges not only teach practical skills but also promote a mindset of resilience and resourcefulness. Students should be encouraged to experiment, make mistakes, and learn from those experiences, as this process is essential for developing the ability to innovate and adapt in the face of uncertainty.

Moreover, teaching practical skills should be a community-wide effort, not confined to the young or to formal educational settings. All members of the community, regardless of age, should be involved in the learning process. This might include intergenerational learning, where elders pass down traditional knowledge and skills to younger members, or communal workshops where everyone can learn new techniques together. This inclusive approach ensures that knowledge is widely distributed and that everyone has the opportunity to contribute to the community's survival and rebuilding efforts.

The focus on practical skills does not mean abandoning intellectual or creative pursuits. Instead, these skills should be integrated into a broader educational framework that also values critical thinking, creativity, and cultural preservation. For instance, students learning about agriculture might also study the science behind soil health and crop rotation, or those learning construction might explore the principles of engineering and architecture. By blending practical skills with intellectual inquiry, the community can foster a well-rounded education that prepares individuals to not only survive but to rebuild a thriving, sustainable society.

In summary, teaching practical skills is an essential part of education in a post-collapse world. By prioritizing survival skills, incorporating hands-on learning, and encouraging problem-solving and innovation, communities can equip their members with the tools they need to rebuild and thrive. This approach not only ensures that the community can meet its immediate needs but also lays the foundation for long-term resilience and self-sufficiency, empowering individuals to take an active role in the ongoing effort to rebuild and improve their world.

9.3 Science and Technology for the Future

In the wake of a societal collapse, the preservation and advancement of science and technology become crucial for the long-term survival and growth of any community. While the immediate focus may be on survival and rebuilding basic infrastructure, it is essential not to lose sight of the role that science and technology play in shaping a sustainable and resilient future. Understanding and applying the basic principles of science and engineering, encouraging experimentation and technological adaptation, and working toward the reconstruction of essential technological infrastructure are key steps in ensuring that communities can not only survive but also thrive in the post-collapse world.

The foundation of science and technology education in a post-collapse environment lies in teaching the basic principles of science and engineering. Even in the absence of advanced tools and laboratories, these principles can be conveyed through simple, practical experiments and observations that demonstrate the underlying concepts. For example, lessons on physics can be taught by exploring basic mechanics through the construction of simple machines like levers and pulleys, which can then be applied to real-world tasks such as lifting heavy objects or constructing buildings. Chemistry can be introduced through the creation of rudimentary batteries or the fermentation process, demonstrating how chemical reactions can be harnessed for energy and food preservation. Biology lessons might focus on understanding ecosystems, the principles of sustainable agriculture, or the basics of human anatomy and health.

By grounding scientific education in practical, hands-on experiences, communities can ensure that their members develop a functional understanding of these concepts and are able to apply them in their daily lives. This approach not only helps preserve scientific knowledge but also empowers individuals to think critically and solve problems using the resources available to them. In this way, science education becomes directly relevant to the community's survival and development, rather than being seen as an abstract or distant field of study.

Encouraging experimentation and technological adaptation is another crucial element of science and technology education. In a world where the technological landscape has drastically changed, communities must be able to adapt existing technologies to new circumstances or develop entirely new solutions to meet their needs. This requires a mindset of curiosity and innovation, where experimentation is encouraged and failure is seen as a learning opportunity rather than a setback. Communities should foster a culture of tinkering and problem-solving, where individuals feel empowered to modify tools, invent new devices, or repurpose materials in creative ways.

For example, the community might experiment with alternative energy sources, such as designing small-scale wind turbines or solar collectors using scavenged materials. They could explore ways to improve agricultural productivity through the development of simple irrigation systems or experiment with new methods of food preservation that extend the shelf life of perishable goods. By encouraging these kinds of projects, the community not only develops practical solutions to immediate challenges but also builds a base of technological knowledge that can be expanded upon as resources and capabilities grow.

It is also important to recognize that science and technology education should not be limited to those with a formal background in these fields. In a post-collapse world, every member of the community can contribute to the advancement of technology through their unique experiences and perspectives. Farmers, builders, and artisans all possess valuable knowledge that can be integrated into scientific and technological endeavors. This inclusive approach ensures that the community's efforts are grounded in practical reality and that innovations are accessible and relevant to everyone.

Rebuilding essential technological infrastructure is the ultimate goal of science and technology education in a post-collapse scenario. While it may not be possible to immediately restore all the conveniences of modern life, communities can work toward reestablishing key technologies that enhance their quality of life and support their long-term sustainability. This might include the construction of basic communication systems, such as radio networks that allow for coordination with neighboring communities, or the development of water purification systems that ensure a safe and reliable supply of drinking water. In the realm of agriculture, the community could focus on developing more efficient tools for planting and harvesting crops or constructing greenhouses that extend the growing season.

The reconstruction of technological infrastructure should be approached with an eye toward sustainability and resilience. Rather than simply trying to replicate the technologies of the pre-collapse world, communities should consider how these systems can be improved to better suit the current environment. This might involve using renewable energy sources, designing technologies that are easily repairable with available materials, or developing systems that are scalable and adaptable to different conditions. By taking this approach, communities not only rebuild their technological capabilities but also ensure that these systems are robust and capable of evolving over time.

Furthermore, science and technology education can play a critical role in fostering a sense of hope and progress within the community. In a world where the future is uncertain, the ability to innovate and create new technologies can provide a sense of agency and control. It reminds the community that, despite the challenges they face, they have the power to shape their own destiny and improve their circumstances through knowledge and ingenuity. This forward-looking perspective is essential for maintaining morale and motivation, as it reinforces the idea that the community is not merely surviving but actively working toward a better future.

In conclusion, science and technology are integral to the long-term success of any community in a post-collapse world. By teaching the basic principles of science and engineering, encouraging experimentation and technological adaptation, and focusing on the reconstruction of essential technological infrastructure, communities can build a foundation for sustainable growth and resilience. This approach not only preserves valuable knowledge but also empowers individuals to take an active role in rebuilding and improving their world, ensuring that the community is well-equipped to face the challenges of the future.

Chapter 10: Reconnecting with Nature

Nature is both a provider and a protector. In this chapter, learn how to restore natural ecosystems, practice sustainable agriculture, and prepare for environmental challenges to ensure a harmonious relationship with the environment.

10.1 Restoring Natural Ecosystems

In a post-collapse world, the relationship between humans and the natural environment must be redefined and nurtured. Restoring natural ecosystems is a critical step in this process, as healthy ecosystems are the foundation upon which communities can rebuild sustainably. A thriving environment not only provides essential resources such as clean water, fertile soil, and food, but it also offers protection against natural disasters and climate extremes. Engaging in reforestation, habitat restoration projects, and protecting local wildlife and biodiversity are vital actions that help repair the damage caused by human activity and ensure that the environment can support future generations.

Reforestation is one of the most impactful ways to restore natural ecosystems. Forests play a crucial role in maintaining the planet's health by regulating the climate, stabilizing the soil, and providing habitat for countless species. In many areas, deforestation has left the land barren and vulnerable to erosion, floods, and the loss of biodiversity. By planting trees and restoring forests, communities can begin to reverse this damage. The process involves more than simply planting trees; it requires careful planning to ensure that the right species are selected for the specific ecosystem, that they are planted in a way that mimics natural growth patterns, and that the forest is allowed to regenerate naturally over time. Reforestation efforts should prioritize native species that are well-adapted to the local environment, as these plants will be more resilient and provide better support for local wildlife.

Habitat restoration goes hand in hand with reforestation, as it involves the broader task of rehabilitating entire ecosystems, including wetlands, grasslands, and coastal areas. These ecosystems are often overlooked but are just as important as forests in maintaining ecological balance. Wetlands, for example, act as natural water filtration systems and flood buffers, while coastal ecosystems such as mangroves protect against storm surges and erosion. Restoring these habitats involves removing invasive species, reintroducing native plants and animals, and sometimes re-engineering the landscape to restore natural water flows or soil conditions. The goal is to create a self-sustaining ecosystem that can support a wide range of species and provide valuable ecosystem services to the community.

Protecting local wildlife and biodiversity is another essential aspect of restoring natural ecosystems. Biodiversity is the web of life that underpins the health of the planet; it ensures ecosystem resilience, provides genetic resources for food and medicine, and supports cultural and recreational activities. In a post-collapse scenario, where many species may already be threatened by habitat loss, pollution, and climate change, it is vital to take active measures to protect and preserve local wildlife. This can involve creating wildlife corridors that connect fragmented habitats, establishing protected areas where hunting and development are prohibited, and engaging in species recovery programs for endangered animals and plants. Communities should also be educated about the importance of biodiversity and the ways in which they can coexist with local wildlife, such as by minimizing human-wildlife conflicts and avoiding the use of harmful chemicals that can poison the environment.

Sustainable hunting and fishing practices are also crucial to maintaining the balance of natural ecosystems. In many traditional societies, hunting and fishing are integral parts of the local culture and economy. However, without proper management, these activities can lead to overexploitation and the collapse of wildlife populations. Sustainable practices involve setting limits on the number of animals that can be hunted or fish that can be caught, ensuring that only certain species are targeted while others are protected, and using methods that minimize environmental impact. For example, selective fishing techniques can help avoid the bycatch of non-target species, and community-managed hunting zones can ensure that wildlife populations remain healthy and sustainable. By adopting these practices, communities can continue to benefit from the natural resources around them without compromising the health of the ecosystem.

In summary, restoring natural ecosystems is a multifaceted effort that requires reforestation, habitat restoration, wildlife protection, and sustainable resource management. These actions are not just about healing the land but also about creating a harmonious relationship between humans and nature that can support both ecological and human health for generations to come. By investing in the restoration and protection of natural ecosystems, communities can build a stronger, more resilient foundation for their future.

10.2 Sustainable Agriculture and Permaculture

As communities seek to reconnect with nature in the aftermath of societal collapse, sustainable agriculture and permaculture practices offer a way to produce food that is not only efficient but also harmonious with the environment. Unlike conventional farming, which often relies on monocultures, chemical fertilizers, and pesticides, sustainable agriculture and permaculture focus on creating agricultural systems that mimic the complexity and resilience of natural ecosystems. This approach not only improves soil health and increases biodiversity but also reduces the need for external inputs, making the community more self-reliant and environmentally friendly.

Permaculture is a design philosophy that seeks to create self-sustaining agricultural systems by integrating plants, animals, and people in ways that are mutually beneficial. At its core, permaculture is about observing and mimicking the patterns found in nature to create agricultural systems that are resilient, sustainable, and productive. For example, instead of planting a single crop in a large field, a permaculture garden might include a diverse mix of plants that support each other in various ways—some fixing nitrogen in the soil, others attracting pollinators, and still others providing ground cover to retain moisture and prevent erosion. This diversity not only makes the system more resilient to pests and diseases but also ensures that it can continue to produce food year after year without depleting the soil.

One of the key principles of permaculture is the integration of animals and plants into a sustainable cycle. Animals play an essential role in maintaining the health of a permaculture system by providing manure, which enriches the soil, and by controlling pests. For example, chickens can be used to clear fields of weeds and insects while simultaneously fertilizing the soil with their droppings. Similarly, ducks can be introduced into rice paddies to eat pests and aerate the water, reducing the need for chemical pesticides and fertilizers. By integrating animals into the farming system in a way that mimics their natural roles, permaculture not only increases the efficiency of food production but also creates a more balanced and sustainable ecosystem.

Creating food forests is another powerful technique used in permaculture to develop sustainable gardens. A food forest is a multi-layered garden that mimics a natural forest, with different plants occupying different levels or "strata." This includes tall fruit and nut trees forming the canopy, smaller trees and shrubs in the understory, herbs and vegetables at ground level, and root crops underground. The diverse plant species in a food forest work together to create a stable and productive ecosystem that requires minimal maintenance. The trees provide shade and reduce the need for irrigation, the shrubs attract beneficial insects, and the ground cover helps retain moisture and prevent weeds. Over time, a well-designed food forest can produce a wide variety of fruits, nuts, vegetables, and herbs with little or no need for artificial inputs.

In addition to food forests, sustainable gardens can take many forms, depending on the needs and resources of the community. Raised bed gardens, for example, are an excellent option in areas with poor soil or limited space, as they allow for better control over soil quality and drainage. Companion planting—growing certain plants together because they benefit each other—can also enhance productivity and reduce the need for chemical inputs. For instance, planting marigolds alongside tomatoes can help deter pests, while beans planted with corn can fix nitrogen in the soil, benefiting both crops. By incorporating these sustainable practices, communities can create gardens that are not only productive but also ecologically sound.

Moreover, sustainable agriculture and permaculture are not just about growing food; they are also about building a deeper connection between people and the land. These practices encourage communities to work with nature rather than against it, fostering a sense of stewardship and respect for the environment. They also promote self-reliance, as communities learn to produce their own food in a way that is both sustainable and resilient to environmental challenges. In a post-collapse world, where external resources may be scarce or unreliable, the ability to produce food sustainably is crucial for long-term survival.

In conclusion, sustainable agriculture and permaculture offer a holistic approach to food production that integrates the principles of ecology with the practical needs of the community. By designing agricultural systems that mimic natural ecosystems, integrating animals and plants into sustainable cycles, and creating food forests and sustainable gardens, communities can ensure a steady supply of food while also protecting and enhancing the environment. These practices not only provide immediate benefits in terms of food security but also contribute to the long-term resilience and sustainability of the community as a whole.

10.3 Preparing for Environmental Challenges

In a post-collapse world, the ability to anticipate and respond to environmental challenges is critical for the survival and resilience of any community. As the global climate continues to change, and as natural disasters become more frequent and severe, communities must develop strategies to mitigate these risks and adapt to new environmental realities. Preparing for environmental challenges involves a deep understanding of climate-related risks, proactive planning for natural disasters and extreme weather, and fostering community resilience to environmental changes. By taking these steps, communities can protect themselves against the unpredictable forces of nature and ensure their long-term sustainability.

Understanding and mitigating climate-related risks is the first step in preparing for environmental challenges. Climate change has led to an increase in the frequency and intensity of extreme weather events, such as hurricanes, floods, droughts, and wildfires. These events can have devastating effects on communities, particularly those that are already vulnerable due to limited resources or geographic location. To effectively prepare for these risks, communities must first conduct a thorough assessment of their local environment, identifying the specific threats they are most likely to face. This might involve studying historical weather patterns, monitoring changes in local ecosystems, and consulting with experts or other communities that have faced similar challenges.

Once the risks have been identified, the next step is to develop strategies for mitigating them. This might include building infrastructure that is resilient to extreme weather, such as flood barriers, wind-resistant shelters, or firebreaks. For example, in areas prone to flooding, communities might construct levees, create retention ponds, or restore wetlands to absorb excess water. In regions at risk of wildfires, clearing brush and creating firebreaks can help prevent the spread of fires, while building homes with fire-resistant materials can reduce the damage if a fire does occur. Communities should also consider the long-term impacts of climate change, such as rising sea levels or changing precipitation patterns, and plan accordingly. This might involve relocating vulnerable populations, diversifying water sources, or transitioning to crops that are better suited to the new climate conditions.

Preparing for natural disasters and extreme weather is another critical aspect of environmental resilience. In a post-collapse world, where external assistance may be unavailable or delayed, communities must be self-reliant in responding to emergencies. This requires the development of comprehensive disaster preparedness plans that include clear protocols for evacuation, emergency communication, and the distribution of supplies. These plans should be regularly reviewed and updated to reflect new information or changes in the environment. Drills and simulations are also essential for ensuring that all community members know how to respond in an emergency. For example, practicing evacuation routes, setting up temporary shelters, and conducting search and rescue exercises can help build confidence and coordination among community members.

In addition to physical preparations, communities should also invest in building social resilience to environmental challenges. This involves fostering strong social networks, promoting cooperation, and ensuring that all members of the community have access to the resources and support they need to recover from disasters. In the aftermath of a natural disaster, social cohesion can make a significant difference in the speed and effectiveness of recovery efforts. Communities that are united, where members trust and support one another, are better able to pool resources, share information, and rebuild together. This social resilience is just as important as physical resilience in ensuring the long-term survival of the community.

Developing community resilience to environmental changes also requires a proactive approach to adaptation. As the environment changes, communities must be willing to adapt their practices, technologies, and lifestyles to the new conditions. This might involve transitioning to more sustainable agricultural practices that are better suited to the changing climate, such as drought-resistant crops or agroforestry systems that enhance soil moisture and reduce the need for irrigation. It could also involve adopting new technologies, such as rainwater harvesting systems or solar-powered desalination plants, to ensure a reliable supply of clean water in regions where traditional water sources are becoming scarce. Communities should also consider the impact of climate change on local biodiversity and take steps to protect and restore ecosystems that provide essential services, such as pollination, water filtration, and carbon sequestration.

Education and awareness are key components of building resilience to environmental challenges. Community members need to be informed about the risks they face and the steps they can take to protect themselves and their environment. This might involve workshops, training sessions, or public information campaigns that teach people how to prepare for natural disasters, reduce their environmental footprint, and adapt to changing conditions. It is also important to involve the community in the decision-making process, ensuring that everyone has a voice in shaping the strategies and policies that will affect their future. By fostering a culture of environmental awareness and stewardship, communities can build a strong foundation for resilience that will serve them well in the face of future challenges.

In summary, preparing for environmental challenges in a post-collapse world requires a multifaceted approach that includes understanding and mitigating climate-related risks, preparing for natural disasters and extreme weather, and developing community resilience to environmental changes. By taking proactive steps to protect themselves and their environment, communities can reduce their vulnerability to the unpredictable forces of nature and ensure their long-term survival and prosperity. This holistic approach not only enhances the community's ability to withstand environmental shocks but also empowers them to adapt and thrive in a rapidly changing world.

Conclusion

Reflecting on the Journey

As we reach the conclusion of this comprehensive guide, it is essential to take a moment to reflect on the journey we have embarked upon together. This journey has not only been about acquiring the knowledge and skills necessary to survive and rebuild in a post-collapse world but also about understanding the deeper principles that underpin a thriving and resilient society. Throughout the ten chapters, we have explored the critical aspects of survival, sustainability, governance, and community building, all of which are essential for creating a new civilization that is stronger, more sustainable, and more equitable than the one that came before.

The first chapter laid the groundwork for survival in the immediate aftermath of a societal collapse. We began by understanding the common causes of such collapses, the signs that indicate an impending breakdown, and the psychological impact on individuals and communities. The focus then shifted to the essential survival needs: securing water sources, finding or constructing shelter, and ensuring an adequate food supply. We also discussed the importance of self-defense and security in a world where traditional law enforcement may no longer be reliable, and we highlighted the need for basic medical preparedness, including first aid skills and creating a medical kit. The chapter concluded with the formation of a survival group, emphasizing that community is a critical factor in survival.

In the second chapter, we turned our attention to establishing a sustainable food supply, recognizing that long-term survival depends on the ability to produce and preserve food. We delved into gardening for survival, selecting crops that thrive in various climates, and employing techniques to maximize yield with limited resources. Foraging and hunting were explored as supplementary food sources, with an emphasis on identifying edible wild plants and basic hunting and trapping techniques. Animal husbandry was discussed as a means of creating a stable food source, with guidance on choosing the right livestock and maintaining their shelters. Finally, we covered various food preservation techniques, such as canning, pickling, dehydration, and root cellaring, to ensure that food supplies last through difficult times.

Chapter three focused on building and maintaining shelter, one of the most fundamental aspects of survival. We began by discussing the strategic considerations for selecting a safe location, assessing natural resources and risks, and zoning a community for optimal functionality. Basic construction techniques were introduced, with practical advice on building sturdy, weather-resistant structures using available materials. The chapter also covered advanced building techniques, including the use of sustainable materials like earthbags, cob, and straw bales, and the integration of renewable energy sources. Maintenance and repairs were highlighted as ongoing tasks to ensure the longevity of shelters, and we discussed creating safe and comfortable living spaces that also contribute to mental well-being.

Water management and sanitation were the focus of the fourth chapter, recognizing that access to clean water and proper waste management are critical to preventing disease and maintaining health. We explored methods for finding and purifying water, such as locating water sources in the wild and setting up rainwater collection systems. Building water systems, including wells, cisterns, and gravity-fed systems, was discussed in detail, along with irrigation techniques for sustainable agriculture. Waste management and sanitation practices, such as composting toilets and greywater systems, were emphasized as essential to maintaining a healthy community. The chapter concluded with a discussion on community water infrastructure, including equitable distribution and the management of communal water resources.

Chapter five addressed the reestablishment of communication and transportation networks, vital for connecting isolated communities and facilitating the exchange of goods and information. We began with emergency communication systems, including basic radio operation, setting up local communication networks, and using non-verbal communication methods like Morse code. The chapter then explored the rebuilding of transportation networks, with practical advice on clearing and maintaining roads, alternative transportation methods, and setting up a community transport system. Signaling for help, an essential skill in emergencies, was also covered, with guidance on creating effective visual and auditory signals. Finally, we discussed long-distance travel and exploration, including navigation techniques and the creation of simple maps.

In chapter six, we delved into power and energy solutions, recognizing that access to energy is crucial for maintaining a functioning community. We explored the potential of harnessing solar energy through the construction and maintenance of solar panels, solar water heaters, and solar cookers. Wind and water power were also discussed as alternative energy sources, with practical advice on building wind turbines, water wheels, and micro-hydro systems. The chapter covered bioenergy and sustainable fuels, including the production of biofuels and the use of biogas digesters. Energy storage solutions, such as battery systems and thermal mass storage, were highlighted as essential for managing energy supply, and we concluded with energy conservation strategies to reduce energy needs and ensure sustainability.

Chapter seven shifted focus to the social structures necessary for a thriving community, beginning with the establishment of leadership. We discussed identifying natural leaders, creating a governance council, and developing decision-making processes that encourage participation. The creation of laws and regulations was explored, with an emphasis on establishing a code of conduct, enforcing rules fairly, and adapting laws as the community grows. Building a resilient culture was highlighted as a key component of social stability, with discussions on celebrating community achievements, promoting cooperation and sustainability, and fostering the arts and literature that reflect the new society.

In chapter eight, we addressed health and medicine in a new world, recognizing that maintaining health is fundamental to survival. We began by discussing the establishment of a community health system, including training healthcare providers, setting up clinics, and establishing a medical supply chain. The chapter then explored traditional and herbal medicine as valuable resources in a world where modern medicine may be scarce. Preventive healthcare and hygiene were emphasized as critical to preventing disease, with practical advice on sanitation, vaccination, and promoting healthy lifestyles. Finally, we covered emergency medical response, including training for common medical emergencies, creating a network of first responders, and developing protocols for disease outbreaks.

Chapter nine focused on education and knowledge preservation, recognizing that the transmission of knowledge is crucial for rebuilding civilization. We discussed establishing a learning environment through the creation of makeshift classrooms, recruiting educators, and designing a curriculum focused on survival and rebuilding. Teaching practical skills, such as farming, construction, and problem-solving, was emphasized as essential for equipping community members with the tools they need to contribute to the rebuilding effort. Finally, we explored the importance of science and technology for the future, encouraging experimentation and technological adaptation, and working toward the reconstruction of essential technological infrastructure.

In the final chapter, chapter ten, we explored the importance of reconnecting with nature as a foundation for sustainable living. We began by discussing the restoration of natural ecosystems through reforestation, habitat restoration, and the protection of local wildlife and biodiversity. Sustainable agriculture and permaculture were highlighted as key practices for creating food systems that are in harmony with nature. The chapter also covered preparing for environmental challenges, with practical advice on understanding climate-related risks, preparing for natural disasters, and developing community resilience to environmental changes.

The Importance of Community

Throughout this journey, one theme has remained constant: the importance of community. Rebuilding civilization is not an individual endeavor; it is a collective effort that requires the collaboration, support, and mutual aid of every member of the community. The challenges of a post-collapse world are too great for any one person to overcome alone, and it is through the strength of community that we find the resilience and resources needed to rebuild.

In each chapter, we have seen how the involvement of the community is crucial to success. Whether it is forming a survival group in the immediate aftermath of a collapse, establishing a sustainable food supply, building and maintaining shelter, or reestablishing communication and transportation networks, the collective effort of the community is what makes these endeavors possible. Community members bring diverse skills, knowledge, and perspectives, and when these are pooled together, they create a powerful force for survival and progress.

Community is also the foundation of social structures, governance, and culture. As we discussed in chapter seven, establishing leadership and creating laws requires the participation and support of the entire community. Building a resilient culture, promoting values of cooperation and sustainability, and fostering the arts and literature that reflect the new society are all efforts that depend on the active engagement of the community. It is through these shared endeavors that a sense of solidarity and belonging is created, which is essential for the long-term stability and prosperity of the community.

In the realm of health and medicine, the community plays a vital role in maintaining health and preventing disease. The establishment of a community health system, the practice of traditional and herbal medicine, and the promotion of preventive healthcare and hygiene all rely on the collective effort of the community. In times of emergency, it is the community that comes together to provide care, support, and resources to those in need.

Education and knowledge preservation are also deeply rooted in the community. As we discussed in chapter nine, the transmission of knowledge is a collective responsibility. Educators, parents, elders, and community members all contribute to the education of the younger generation, ensuring that essential skills, knowledge, and values are passed down. Science and technology, too, are advanced through the collaborative efforts of the community, as individuals share their expertise, experiment with new ideas, and work together to rebuild technological infrastructure.

Finally, in reconnecting with nature, the community plays a central role in restoring natural ecosystems, practicing sustainable agriculture, and preparing for environmental challenges. These efforts require the participation of every member of the community, as the health of the environment is directly linked to the well-being of the community. By working together to protect and restore the natural world, communities can create a sustainable future for themselves and future generations.

The importance of community cannot be overstated. It is through the strength of community that we find the resilience, resources, and support needed to rebuild civilization. Rebuilding civilization is not just about surviving; it is about thriving, and this is only possible when we work together, support one another, and build a society based on the principles of cooperation, mutual aid, and shared responsibility.

Looking to the Future

As we look to the future, we envision a new society built on the principles of sustainability, resilience, and cooperation. This new society is not a return to the old ways but a reimagining of what civilization can be. It is a society that learns from the mistakes of the past, that values the health of the planet as much as the health of its people, and that prioritizes the well-being of the community over individual gain.

In this new society, sustainability is at the core of every decision. The lessons learned from the collapse teach us that the unchecked exploitation of resources, the disregard for the environment, and the focus on short-term profits over long-term sustainability are paths to disaster. In the new society, sustainable practices are not just encouraged; they are essential. Whether it is in agriculture, energy production, construction, or governance, every decision is made with the understanding that the future of the community depends on the health of the environment.

Resilience is another key principle of the new society. The collapse has shown us that the systems we once relied on are fragile and vulnerable to disruption. In the new society, resilience is built into every aspect of life. This means creating systems that are flexible, adaptable, and capable of withstanding shocks and stresses. It means fostering a culture of innovation and problem-solving, where challenges are seen as opportunities to grow and improve. It also means building strong social networks and a sense of community that can provide support in times of crisis.

Cooperation is the third pillar of the new society. The collapse has taught us that we are stronger together than we are alone. In the new society, cooperation is not just a strategy; it is a value that is deeply ingrained in the culture. Whether it is working together to produce food, build shelter, or protect the environment, cooperation is seen as the key to success. This spirit of cooperation extends beyond the boundaries of individual communities, fostering collaboration and mutual support between different groups and regions.

As a reader, you have played a crucial role in this journey. By engaging with the content of this book, you have taken the first steps toward becoming a leader, a teacher, and a builder of the new society. The knowledge and skills you have acquired are not just tools for survival;

they are the building blocks of a better future. You have the power to shape this future, to influence the direction of your community, and to contribute to the creation of a society that is more just, more sustainable, and more resilient than the one that came before.

Your role in shaping this future is not limited to your actions in the present. As you continue to learn, grow, and adapt, you will become a source of knowledge and inspiration for others. You will have the opportunity to teach, to lead, and to mentor the next generation of builders and thinkers. Your experiences, your successes, and even your failures will contribute to the collective wisdom of the community, helping to guide future decisions and actions.

In looking to the future, it is important to remember that the journey of rebuilding civilization is not a linear path. There will be setbacks, challenges, and moments of doubt. But it is in these moments that the true strength of the community will be revealed. By staying committed to the principles of sustainability, resilience, and cooperation, and by supporting one another through the ups and downs, the community can overcome any obstacle and continue to move forward.

As we envision this new society, it is also important to recognize that the work of rebuilding is never truly complete. The world is constantly changing, and the challenges of today will not be the challenges of tomorrow. The new society must be dynamic, capable of evolving and adapting to new circumstances. This requires a mindset of continuous learning and improvement, where every member of the community is encouraged to contribute ideas, to experiment, and to innovate. It also requires a commitment to inclusivity, ensuring that all voices are heard, and that everyone has a role to play in shaping the future.

In conclusion, looking to the future is about more than just survival; it is about creating a world that reflects the best of what humanity can achieve. It is about building a society that is sustainable, resilient, and cooperative, where the health of the planet and the well-being of the community are at the forefront of every decision. As a reader, you have the knowledge, the skills, and the power to shape this future. The journey may be challenging, but it is also filled with opportunities to create something truly extraordinary. Together, we can build a world that is not only capable of surviving but also of thriving for generations to come.

Final Words of Encouragement

As we conclude this journey, it is important to leave you with a sense of hope, purpose, and empowerment. The task of rebuilding civilization is monumental, but it is not insurmountable. Throughout history, humanity has faced countless challenges, and time and again, we have risen to the occasion. The resilience, creativity, and determination that have carried us through the darkest of times are the same qualities that will guide us as we rebuild.

The power of individual and collective action cannot be overstated. Every action you take, no matter how small, contributes to the greater goal of rebuilding civilization. Whether you are planting a garden, teaching a child, constructing a shelter, or leading a community, your efforts matter. You are part of a larger movement, a global effort to create a better, more sustainable world. And as you take these actions, you inspire others to do the same, creating a ripple effect that spreads far beyond your immediate surroundings.

Remember that you are not alone on this journey. The challenges you face are shared by communities around the world, and the solutions you develop can inspire and support others. Collaboration and mutual support are key to overcoming the obstacles ahead. By working together, sharing knowledge, and learning from one another, we can achieve far more than we ever could alone.

As you move forward, it is important to stay focused on the principles that have guided this journey: sustainability, resilience, and cooperation. These principles are not just ideals; they are the foundation upon which the new society will be built. They are the keys to creating a world that is capable of withstanding the challenges of the future and providing a safe, healthy, and fulfilling life for all its members.

In the face of adversity, it is easy to become discouraged, to feel overwhelmed by the enormity of the task ahead. But it is in these moments that you must hold on to hope and remember that every step forward, no matter how small, brings us closer to the world we envision. The journey of rebuilding civilization is not a sprint; it is a marathon, and it is one that we must undertake with patience, perseverance, and a steadfast commitment to our goals.

As you continue on this path, take pride in the progress you have made and the contributions you have given. Celebrate your successes, learn from your failures, and keep moving forward with determination and purpose. The road ahead may be long, but it is also filled with opportunities to create a better world, a world that reflects the best of what humanity can achieve.

In the end, the journey of rebuilding civilization is about more than just survival; it is about creating a legacy for future generations. It is about ensuring that the mistakes of the past are not repeated and that the world we leave behind is one of peace, prosperity, and harmony with the natural world. This is a journey that requires courage, vision, and unwavering commitment, but it is one that is worth undertaking.

So as we close this book, know that the power to shape the future is in your hands. You have the knowledge, the skills, and the determination to make a difference. The journey may be challenging, but it is also filled with potential. Together, we can build a world that is not only capable of surviving but also of thriving for generations to come. The future is yours to create, and it starts with the actions you take today.

Thank you!

We have come to the end of a challenging yet rewarding journey together. Your commitment to delving into the depths of survival strategies, sustainable living practices, and the principles of rebuilding civilization is truly commendable. This book is a reflection of not just my knowledge and experience, but also your dedication to learning and growing in the face of uncertainty.

If this guide has provided you with valuable insights and practical advice, I would be immensely grateful if you could share your thoughts through a review. Your feedback is not only appreciated but vital in helping others find the information they need to prepare for and thrive in any situation.

Thank you for taking this journey toward resilience and self-reliance. Your efforts to embrace these principles contribute to a more sustainable and hopeful future for all. Together, we can build a world that not only survives but flourishes in harmony with our surroundings.

Made in United States
Orlando, FL
06 November 2024